Egerton Ryerson

First Lessons in Christian Morals for Canadian Families and Schools

Egerton Ryerson

First Lessons in Christian Morals for Canadian Families and Schools

ISBN/EAN: 9783337023041

Printed in Europe, USA, Canada, Australia, Japan

Cover: Foto ©Lupo / pixelio.de

More available books at **www.hansebooks.com**

Canadian Series of School Books.

FIRST LESSONS

IN

CHRISTIAN MORALS;

FOR

CANADIAN FAMILIES AND SCHOOLS.

BY

EGERTON RYERSON, D.D., LL.D.

"Never suffer the valuable moments of life to steal by unimproved, and leave thee in idleness and vacancy; but be always reading, or writing, or praying, or meditating, or employed in some useful labour for the common good."—*Kempis.*

"Religion refines our moral sentiments, disengages the heart from every vain desire, renders it tranquil under misfortunes, humble in the presence of God, and steady in the society of man."—*Dr. Johnson.*

Authorized by the Council of Public Instruction of Ontario.

TORONTO:
COPP, CLARK & CO., KING STREET EAST.
1871.

Entered according to Act of the Parliament of Canada, in the year One Thousand Eight Hundred and Seventy-one, by the REV. EGERTON RYERSON, LL.D., Chief Superintendent of Education for Ontario, in the Office of the Minister of Agriculture.

PREFATORY NOTICE.

The following little book of "*First Lessons in Christian Morals*," like the "*First Lessons in Agriculture*," is a gratuitous contribution, on the part of the Author, to an essential branch of education.

The selection and arrangement of topics, the mode of presenting them, together with many of the definitions, explanations, and illustrations, are my own ; but in some instances I have appropriated, what appeared to me, the best thoughts and sometimes the best words of the best authors.

Instead of entering into any of the speculations with which many works on moral science commence, I have, at once, assumed the truth of Christianity and the authority of the Holy Scriptures, and have endeavoured to present the subjects in harmony with the views of all religious persuasions who receive the BIBLE as the rule of their faith and practice, and Jesus Christ as the only foundation of their hopes of eternal life.

The want I attempt to supply by this little book has been widely felt, and often expressed in connection with our system of public instruction.

In "*First Lessons in Christian Morals*," I need no apology for taking the BIBLE as the rule and standard ; but under any circumstances, we could appeal to no other book with like advantage ; for, with the late Rev. HENRY MELVILLE. and in his language, "we always recur with delight to the testimony of the DEIST, who, after publicly labouring to disprove Christianity, and to bring Scripture into contempt as a forgery, was found instructing his child from the pages of the New Testament. When taxed with the flagrant inconsistency, his only reply was, that it was necessary to teach the child morality, and that nowhere was there to be found such morality as in the Bible. We thank the Deist for his confession. Whatever our scorn of a man who could be guilty of so foul a dishonesty, seeking to sweep from the earth a volume to which, all the while, himself recurred for the principles of education, we thank him for his testimony, that the morality of Scripture is a morality not elsewhere to be found ; so that, if there were no BIBLE, there would be comparatively no source of instruction in duties and virtue, whose neglect and decline would dislocate the happiness of human society The Deist was right. Deny the divine origin of Scripture and nevertheless you must keep the volume as a kind of text book of morality, if indeed you did not wish the banishment from our houses of all that is lovely and sacred, and breaking up, through the lawlessness of ungovernable passion, of the quiet and beauty which are yet around our families."

TORONTO, August, 1871.

P. S.—Recommendation of the Council of Public Instruction.

Extract from the Minutes of the Council of Public Instruction, 13th Nov. 1871.

The Council of Public Instruction for Ontario, having examined the "First Lessons in Christian Morals for Christian Families and Schools, by the Rev. EGERTON RYERSON, D.D., LL.D.," recommend it for use as designed "in Canadian Families and Public Schools," with the proviso in the case of Schools (as contained in the Consolidated School Act, sec. 128) that

"No person shall require any pupil in any School to read or study in or from any religious book, or to join in any exercise of devotion or religion objected to by his or her parents or guardians; but within this limitation, pupils shall be allowed to receive such religious instruction as their parents and guardians desire, according to any regulations provided for the government of Common Schools."

CONTENTS.

LESSON I.—Christian morals defined; first principles of Christianity; (notes); importance of principles to morals; concurred in by various religious persuasions; how taught in the New Testament. 9–11

LESSON II.—Principles reduced to practice; the ten commandments; how taught in the New Testament; (notes and illustrations); moral and ceremonial law; typical services and worship, how superseded; the moral law, perpetual; how taught in the New Testament..................................11–16

LESSON III.—Classification of our duties; our duties to God—Six; why we should believe in, love, worship, obey God, acknowledge his government and providence in all things, and contentedly submit to His dispensations in regard to our health, circumstances and employments........................16–19

LESSON IV.—Our duty to our neighbour, or to others; duties of parents (to be read and considered by parents—not to be learned by pupils and children); to provide for the maintenance of their children—to educate them—criminality of neglect—religious instruction and moral training of children—should teach by example—should make religion amiable and lovely—should make home happy for children —should fit them for business, and assist in their settlement—not always best to leave them a fortune...20–28

LESSON V.—Duty to our neighbour *(continued)*; duties of children to parents; why children should honour their parents; punishments pronounced by the Scripture on undutiful children; Scripture commendations of dutiful children; limits of obedience. (Notes on the the duties of children to parents); two cases—first case, ingratitude and meanness of educated sons and daughters treating their less educated parents with disrespect; second case of ingratitude and undutifulness of sons not supporting their parents in old age and poverty 28–33

CONTENTS.

LESSON VI.—Duty to our neighbour (*continued*); duty of brothers and sisters; duty of children and young people to each other, and to old people; (notes); on the duty of children and young persons to the aged—Scripture precepts and examples—ancient Romans—in England—ominous signs in the United States—warning to young people in Canada; on the deportment of children and young people to each other...33-55

LESSON VII.—Duties to one's self—self control—temper—passions—appetites—propensities; (notes)—duty of self-control in respect to anger; in respect to passions, appetites, propensities; remedy against them...35-39

LESSON VIII.—Duty to one's self (*continued*); culture of the mind, why, what, how; notes on self-culture and mental improvement.....................................40-43

LESSON IX.—Duty to one's self (*continued*); self consecration—its import; reasons for it; what required in it—Baptism, the Lord's Supper; reasons for; what implied in; how to celebrate the Lord's Supper..44-47

LESSON X.—Duty to one's self (*continued*); veracity—what meant by it; how truth or falsehood may be uttered; why the truth should always be spoken; notes on lying—defined—modes of lying—turpitude of it; truth to be spoken at all times—political lying..47-50

LESSON XI.—Right and wrong; distinctions between right and wrong, how perceived; moral quality of actions consists in the intention; conscience the faculty which discerns and decides upon the moral quality of actions; proofs of its existence. Notes on the Lesson—1. Perception of right and wrong, truth and error; intuitive principles and truths; truths arrived at by reasoning. 2. Remarks on conscience; different definitions of conscience; authority, influence, power of conscience—practical lesson. 3. Remarks on different theories of moral virtue, and of the grounds of moral obligation—all converge in the one point of strengthening moral obligation...50-60

LESSON XII.—Rule of moral obligation; insufficiency of the light of nature; the Holy Scriptures; the Scriptures the rule of moral obligation; why, how, made known to us; in what the light of nature is insufficient. Note on the teachings and insufficiency of the light of nature 60–63

LESSON XIII.—The teaching of the Bible superior to that of natural religion in twelve particulars 63–66

LESSON XIV.—How we know the Bible is the Word of God; ten reasons in proof of it 66–69

LESSON XV.—Miracles; fallacy of Hume's objection to miracles exposed; testimony in proof of miracles; the great miracle of our Lord's Resurrection, proved by an examination of the evidence against and for it; nine reasons in proof of our Lord's resurrection; objection to the *mystery* of the resurrection, and to mystery generally shown to be groundless and absurd. Note on the Infidel's objection not to believe what is mysterious—its unreasonableness and absurdity illustrated and proved.

Notes on the Bible; its character; its influence upon the intellect and heart; its supreme importance and excellence 70–85

LESSON XVI.—Happiness; wherein mankind agree and differ in respect to happiness; reasons why happiness does not consist in riches; nor in pleasures of sense; nor in exalted rank or station; nor in exemption from labour or toil. Four ordinary but essential elements of happiness; four reasons why man's highest perfection and happiness consists in the favour of God and in conformity to His image of righteousness and true holiness. 85–94

FIRST LESSONS IN CHRISTIAN MORALS.

(NOTE.—It is not intended that pupils should learn by heart what is contained in the *Notes*, printed in smaller type; but it is desired that all, both young and old, should read and consider them.)

LESSON I.

CHRISTIAN MORALS: FIRST PRINCIPLES OF CHRISTIANITY.

1. *What are Christian morals?*—Christian morals are those principles and duties which Christianity teaches.

2. *What is Christianity?*—Christianity is the religion of which our Lord Jesus Christ is the author and end; or, it is the doctrines, morals, and manner of worship taught by Christ and his Apostles, as revealed in the New Testament.

3. *Where is Christianity taught?*—Christianity is taught in the BIBLE, which has, "God for its author, truth without mixture of error for its matter, and the eternal salvation of mankind for its end."

4. *What is the first principle in Christianity?*—The first principle in Christianity is faith in God the Father: "I believe in God the Father Almighty, maker of heaven and earth."

5. *What is the second principle in Christianity?*—
—The second principle in Christianity is faith in God the Son and His work for mankind: "I believe in Jesus Christ his only Son our Lord; who was conceived by the Holy Ghost, born of the Virgin Mary, suffered under Pontius Pilate, was crucified, dead and buried; the third day he rose again from the dead; he ascended into heaven, and sitteth on the right hand of God the Father Almighty; from thence he shall come to judge the quick and the dead."

6. *What is the third principle in Christianity?*—
The third principle in Christianity is faith in God the Holy Ghost and his work in fitting us to live rightly on earth, and to be happy in heaven: "I believe in the Holy Ghost; the Holy Catholic (or universal) Church; the communion of Saints; the forgiveness of sins; the resurrection of the body; and the life everlasting. Amen."

(NOTES AND ILLUSTRATIONS.—These principles are to Christian morals what the foundation is to a building, what the tree is to fruit, what the heart is to life. Good principles are essential to a good man. Many professed Christians believe more than these three first principles of faith; but no Christian believes less. These are the Trinity of doctrines from which all scriptural truth flows. At the first meeting of the Evangelical Alliance in America, held in Philadelphia, the ministers and members of various religious denominations, and from various parts of Europe and America,—including Episcopalians, Presbyterians, Methodists, Baptists, Congregationalists, and members of some other churches, repeated aloud and together, as expressing the unity of their faith, their religious belief in the words above quoted, as the three vital principles on which all Christian morals are founded.

2. These principles of faith are clearly taught in the Holy Scriptures. as may be seen by referring to the following passages: Deut. 6: 4, 5. 2 Kings 19: 15. Matt. 1: 23. Luke 1: 30-35. Matt. 27: 2, 35; 28: 5, 6. Luke 24: 50, 51. John 6: 69; 11: 25; 14: 1, 16, 17, 26. Acts 1: 8-11. 1 Cor. 15: 15, 20, 51-55. Rev. 21: 1, 4.

LESSON II.

PRINCIPLES REDUCED TO PRACTICE; THE TEN COMMANDMENTS; HOW TAUGHT IN THE NEW TESTAMENT.

7. *How should we reduce to practice the articles of faith as taught in the preceding lesson?*—Our faith in God the Father should lead us to worship and obey him; our faith in God the Son should lead us to trust in him for all that we need, and to follow his example of obedience, meekness, benevolence, and purity; our faith in God the Holy Ghost should lead us to seek his influence and grace to enlighten our minds, to renew our hearts, to assist and sustain us in duty, in suffering, and against temptation, and to sanctify our nature.

8. *What has God commanded us to do?*—God has given us Ten Commandments, the first four of which teach us our duty towards God, and the last six teach us our duty towards man.

9. *Which are these Ten Commandments?*—The same which were first written by the finger of God on two tablets of stone, and given to Moses, and are

recorded in the **twentieth** chapter of the book of Exodus, in the following words:

"God spake these words, saying, I am the Lord thy God, which brought thee out of the land of Egypt, out of the house of bondage.

I. Thou shalt have no other gods before me.

II. Thou shalt not make unto thee any graven image, or any likeness of anything that is in heaven above, or that is in the earth beneath, or that is in the water under the earth: thou shalt not bow thyself to them, nor serve them: for I the Lord thy God am a jealous God, visiting the sins of the fathers upon the children unto the third and fourth generation of them that hate me; and shewing mercy unto thousands of them that love me and keep my commandments.

III. Thou shalt not take the name of the Lord thy God in vain; for the Lord will not hold him guiltless that taketh his name in vain.

IV. Remember the Sabbath day to keep it holy. Six days shalt thou labour, and do all thy work; but the seventh day is the Sabbath of the Lord thy God. In it thou shalt not do any work, thou, nor thy son, nor thy daughter, nor thy man-servant, nor thy maid-servant, nor thy cattle, nor thy stranger that is within thy gates. For in six days the Lord made heaven and earth, the sea, and all that in them is, and rested the seventh day; wherefore the Lord blessed the seventh day, and hallowed it.

V. Honour thy father and thy mother; that thy days may be long in the land which the Lord thy God giveth thee.

VI. Thou shalt not kill.

VII. Thou shalt not commit adultery.

VIII. Thou shalt not steal.

IX. Thou shalt not bear false witness against thy neighbour.

X. Thou shalt not covet thy neighbour's house, thou shalt not covet thy neighbour's wife, nor his man-servant, nor his maid-servant, nor his ox, nor his ass, nor any thing that is thy neighbour's.

10. *Is this law of the Ten commandments taught in the New Testament as well as in the Old Testament?*—Yes; St. Paul says "the law is holy, and the commandment holy, just and good (Romans, 7 : 12); and our Lord says, "Think not that I am come to destroy the law or the prophets: I am not come to destroy, but to fulfil," Matt. 5 : 17.

11. *How did our Lord sum up the two parts of the whole law of the Ten Commandments?*—He summed them up in the following words: "Thou shalt love the Lord thy God with all thy heart, with all thy soul, and with all thy mind. This is the first and great commandment. And the second is like unto it, Thou shalt love thy neighbour as thyself. On these two commandments hang all the law and the prophets." (Matthew 22: 37–40.)

(NOTES AND ILLUSTRATIONS.—1. The particular name by which the Ten Commandments have been called, is the *Moral Law*, as they contain the substance of all the duties which the Scriptures enjoin upon all mankind. In no human composition, ancient or modern, is so much taught in so few words—words which may be learned in a few hours. The Ten Commandments are also called the *Moral Law*, to distinguish them from the ceremonial laws given by God, through Moses, to the Children of Israel respecting the *ceremonies* of their religious worship, and in regard to their political duties as a nation. The whole of their ceremonial services was introductory to a more simple and spiritual worship, and was typical and a shadow of better things to come. The sacrifices, services and priesthood of that worship pointed to the predicted Messiah and his work, received their fulfilment, and resigning their offices, when Jesus, having offered himself once for all a sacrifice for sin, became the High Priest and King in his Church and Kingdom. See this fully explained in the 8th, 9th and 10th chapters of the Epistle to the Hebrews. BLAIR, in his most eloquent sermon *on the Death of Christ*, has beautifully remarked, "This was the ever-memorable point of time which separated the old and the new world from each other. On the one side of the point of separation, you behold the law, with its priests, its sacrifices, and its rites, retiring from sight. On the other side, you behold the Gospel, with its simple and venerable institutions, coming forward into view. Significantly was the veil of temple rent at this hour; for the glory then departed from between the cherubim. The legal high priest delivered up his Urim and Thummim, his breastplate, his robes, and his incense; and CHRIST stood forth as the great High Priest of all succeeding generations. By that one sacrifice which he now offered, he abolished sacrifices for ever. Altars on which the fire had blazed for ages, were now to smoke no more. Victims were no more to bleed. *Not with the blood of bulls and goats, but with His own blood He now entered into the Holy Place, there to appear in the presence of God for us.*"

2. The *Moral Law*, however,—the law of the Ten Commandments, called, by way of pre-eminence, *The Law*, emanating from the perfections of God and founded upon the wants and relations of mankind, without respect to age or nation, remains, like its Author, the same, yesterday, to-day, and forever. This law was made the basis of all our Lord's teaching. He explained and enforced it in his Sermon on the Mount, (Matt. 5th, 6th and 7th chapters), and in his other discourses; applied its principles and duties to various cases, and explained its spiritual and comprehensive meaning. He showed that murder and adultery were committed in the *heart*, independant of any outward act (Matt. 5: 21—28), and that every man of every nation is our neighbour, (Luke, 10 7) : 9–23. He sums up our duty to our neighbour in these words,— "Whatsoever ye would that men should do unto you, do ye even so to them ; for this is the law and the prophets." (Matt. 7: 12.) For the regulation of our feelings and conduct towards our enemies, our Lord has given us this rule,—" I say unto you, love your enemies, bless them that curse you, do good to them that hate you, and pray for them that despitefully use you and persecute you" (Matt. 5: 44); and he enforces forgiveness of injuries by the consideration, "If ye forgive not men their trespasses, neither will your Father forgive your trespasses," (Matt. 6 : 15). He also teaches us not only implicit trust in Divince Providence (Matt. 6 : 26–34), but also the suffering virtues—"Learn of me ; for I am meek and lowly in heart," (Matt. 11 : 29); "In patience possess ye your souls," (Luke 21 : 9).

3. The whole New Testament is, among other things, an explanation and application of The Law, and contains various precepts for our conduct in different relations of life : such as the conduct of *wives* and *husbands*—"Wives, submit yourselves unto your own husbands, as unto the Lord ; husbands, love your wives, even as Christ also loved the church, and gave himself for it," (Ephesians 5 : 22, 25); the conduct of *Children* and *Parents*,—"Children, obey your parents in the

Lord, for this is right;" "Fathers, provoke not your children to wrath; but bring them up in the nurture and admonition of the Lord," (Ephesians 6: 1, 4); the conduct of servants and masters,—"Servants, be subject to your masters with all fear; not only to the good and gentle, but also to the froward;" Masters give unto your servants that which is just and equal; knowing that ye also have a master in heaven," (1 Peter, 11: 18. Colossians 4: 1).

LESSON III.

CLASSIFICATION OF OUR DUTIES—OUR DUTIES TOWARDS GOD.

12. *How may our duties be classified?*—Our duties may be classified under the three following heads: 1. Our duties towards God; 2. Our duties towards our neigbour, or to others; 3. Our duties to ourselves.

(NOTE.—Strictly speaking, our duties to God include all other duties, as they are all enjoined by Him and for His glory. If we do our whole duty to God, we shall necessarily do our duty to others, or to our neighbours and ourselves. But the division of our duties into three classes is convenient for exposition, and to assist in remembering them.)

13. *What are our duties towards God?*—Our duties towards God are those duties which are enjoined in the first four of the Ten Commandments.

14. *Can you state those duties as explained in other parts of the Holy Scriptures?*—1. The first duty is faith in God, as the only true and living God, and before whom we are to have no other gods. "He that cometh to God, must believe that He is, and

is a rewarder of them that diligently seek Him." (Hebrews 11; 6).

2. **Our second duty is to love God with all our heart,** soul, and strength, as taught by Moses (Deut. 6: 5), and by our Lord (Matt. 22: 37), and throughout the Scriptures.

3. **Our third duty is to** worship God privately and publicly; that **is,** to adore, to thank, to pray to God.

4. **Our fourth duty is to** obey God **at all times** and in all circumstances.

5. **Our fifth duty is to** acknowledge **His government and providence in** all things, small **as well as** great.

6. **Our sixth duty is to submit** contentedly to all God's dispensations in **regard to** our health, **circumstances,** and employments.

15. *Why should you believe in God?*—1. Because He has made and He governs all things. 2. Because He has **revealed Himself in** His Word. 3. Because, without faith in God, I have no hope of future existence, and must view myself and the vast world around me as without a maker and fatherless.

16. *Why should you love God?*—1. Because He is the greatest and **best of** beings,—infinitely wise, **good,** holy and merciful. 2. Because I owe to Him my own being, life, **and all** things I enjoy. 3. Because He has given his only begotten Son to suffer,

and die, and rise again to save me. 4. Because He has commanded me to love Him, and made it my highest happiness to do so.

17. *Why should you worship God?*—Because God has commanded public, family, and **private** worship; and I should *adore* him, because **He** only is eternal, all-powerful, all-knowing, **everywhere present**, and supremely holy, **just** and **good**; I should give Him *thanks*, **because He is my greatest benefactor**, in all **things bodily and spiritual**, temporal and eternal; I should *pray* to **Him**, because I need his **mercy, help and blessing**, and because He has commanded me to pray to Him, **and** has expressly promised, that "every one that asketh receiveth, and he that seeketh findeth, and to him that knocketh it shall be opened."

18. *Why should you obey God at all times and in all circumstances?*—I should **obey** God at all times **and in** all circumstances,—**1. Because** He is my Creator, Benefactor and **Father**, and is possessed of every possible perfection. **I belong to Him as my Creator,** and am dependent upon Him for life and all things. I should, therefore, obey Him as a child should obey a wise and kind father. **2. I should obey** him, because **it is right to obey Him.** His **commands express His will, which is always** right. To disregard His will, at any time or in any circumstances, is to do wrong; and it can never be right for me to do wrong. The Old Testament teaches me to " have respect to all God's commandments; and the New Testament says, "Be ye perfect as your Father which is in heaven is perfect," (Ps. 119: 6. Matt. 5: 48).

19. *Why should you acknowledge God's government and providence in all things?*—Because we do not live in an ungoverned and fatherless world; but "the Most High ruleth in the kingdom of men." "His kingdom ruleth over all," the small as well as the great. He who created the grass and the insects, created also the trees, and men, and angels, and rules over that which He has made, and provides for the wants of all. I am under His eye and care, as much as if I were the only being in the universe; and I should, therefore, acknowledge His government and providence in all my ways, and in all things.

20. *Why should you submit contentedly to all God's dispensations in regard to your health, circumstances and employments?*—I should do so for three reasons: *First*—God knows the future as well as the past, He knows all things; He therefore knows what is best for us. *Second*—His *wisdom* and *goodness* make it certain that He *will* do what is best for us. *Third*—His *power* will accomplish whatever His *wisdom* and *goodness* may direct.

LESSON IV.

OUR DUTY TO OUR NEIGHBOUR, OR TO OTHERS; DUTY OF PARENTS.

(NOTE.—When our Lord was asked by one, "Who is my neighbour?" He answered by relating the parable of the Good Samaritan (Luke 10: 29-37), which teaches that every one of every nation is our neighbour, to whom we should exercise offices of kindness, and do as we would be done by. The first duty to our neighbour,—both in the order of nature and of time,—is that of parents to children. The object of these First Lessions is the instruction of children and young people; but I think it would be a serious omission, not to make some reference to the duties of parents. To this subject I devote the following Lesson, which is not intended for youth or to be taught in schools, but is recommended to the careful perusal and consideration of parents.)

1. Marriage was instituted by God himself in the time of man's innocency; and the first Divine institution of society is that of the Family—antecedent to that of the State or of the Church—the origin of all domestic relations, and of all civil society, and on which the continuance and progress of our race depend.

2. At the head of the family stand the *Parents;* and on the manner in which they perform their duties depend not only the welfare of their offspring, but the interests of the state, and of civilization. It has been well said, that "The family is but the nursery for higher and broader spheres of action. In it are to be planted the seeds, and to be nurtured the germs, which are to have their full development, and to bear their fruit, in future years, and in other worlds."

3. The *first* duty of parents is to provide for the *maintenance* of their children. The helplessness of children makes it necessary that some person maintain them; and the duty of doing so is imposed upon parents by natural relation and affection, as well as by the requirements of human and Divine laws. The teaching of the Scriptures on this point is summed up in the memorable words: "If any provide not for his own, especially those of his own household, he hath denied the faith, and is worse than an infidel," (1 Tim. 5: 8); that is, he has practically renounced and disgraced the Christian profession, and neglected a duty which even infidels acknowledge. Hence the guilt of those parents who desert their families, or, in consequence of idleness or drunkenness, expose them to hunger and nakedness, and throw them as paupers upon others for support. The manner in which parents should provide for the maintenance of their children, must depend upon the circumstances of the family. The poor man cannot provide the same food and clothing for his children as the rich man. A parent does his duty when he provides for the support of his children according to his ability, though he may not be able to bring up his children in the affluence which others can command. It may, however, be remarked, that the simple habits of frugality and industry, taught by the lessons of honest poverty, are often in themselves of greater value to children, as experience shows, than wealth and its usual accompaniments.

4. The *second* duty of parents is the *education* of their children. This involves two things: First, their *intellectual* culture, or school training, so as to fit them for their destined employments of life; secondly, their *religious* instruction, or moral training, so as to dispose or fit them to lead a life of honest and Christian men. Our Legislature has thrown the shield of legal protection over children in regard to their elementary school education, by imposing a penalty upon any parent who shall wilfully refuse or neglect to give his child at least four months' school education each year, from the age of seven to twelve years inclusive. Paley truly remarks, that "In *civilized* life, everything is effected by *art* and *skill*. Whence a person who is provided with neither, (and neither can be acquired without exercise and instruction), will be useless; and he that is useless will generally be at the same time mischievous to the community. So that to send an uneducated child into the world is injurious to the rest of mankind; it is little better than to turn out a mad dog or a wild beast into the streets."

5. But if it is criminal in any of the inferior classes of the community to leave their children altogether uneducated, not to inure them to industry or labour, but suffer them to grow up in idleness and vagrancy, it is scarcely less criminal for any of the higher classes not to educate their children, both by habits of industry and attainments, so as to be able and disposed to provide for their own support. Among the ancient Athenians, if the parent did not

educate a child to get a livelihood, the child was not bound to provide for the parent when old and poor. "A man of fortune," says Paley, "who permits his son to consume the season of education in hunting, shooting, or in frequenting horse races, assemblies, or other unedifying, if not vicious diversions, defrauds the community of a benefactor, and bequeaths them a nuisance."

6. The second part of the education of children relates to their *religious instruction and moral training*. Children are not only physical beings, and need food and raiment for their bodies; they are not only intellectual beings, and need mental culture and development; they are also moral and immortal beings, and need that spiritual and moral training which will qualify them to do God's will on earth and partake of his glory in heaven. If the parent has "denied the faith and is worse than an infidel," who neglects to provide material food and raiment for his household, still worse must he be who provides for them no spiritual food and raiment. The command of God by Moses, in his last discourse to his countrymen, was—"These words which I command thee this day, shall be in thine heart; and thou shalt diligently teach unto thy children" (Deut. 6: 6, 7). The same duty is taught in the last chaper of the Apostle Paul's Epistle to the Ephesians, as well as throughout the Scriptures: "Ye fathers, provoke not your children to wrath; but bring them up in the *nurture* and *admonition* of the Lord." (Eph. 6: 4.)

7. The religious instruction and moral training of children involves, briefly,—1. Teaching them their duties towards God and man. 2. The checking and restraining of all evil desires and propensities of their nature. 3. The fostering of all pure, noble, generous sentiments and principles of action. 4. The vigilent guarding them against all evil and seductive influences to which childhood and youth are exposed. 5. All the nameless and mighty influences of a well-ordered and happy religious home. 6. Prayer with and for children, and for the Divine assistance and blessing upon all the efforts employed for making them "members of Christ, children of God, and inheritors of the kingdom of heaven."

8. Two methods by which parents may promote the best religious and temporal interests of their children, deserve special notice. The first is, *their own example*. Parental example teaches more powerfully than parental precept; and the precept is more than paralysed when contradicted by the example. Children can understand acts better than words, while actions speak louder than words. For instance, if a father, with apparent solemnity and earnestness, warns his son against profaneness, or sabbath-breaking, or idleness, or excess in drinking, or bad company, or extravagance, and yet himself profanes God's name, or breaks God's Sabbath, or loiters about without employment, or drinks to excess, or goes into profligate company, or misspends his money, how can even a child fail to see through such mockery? What can the son think but that

his father is counterfeiting virtue, and does not believe what he is saying? Or if a mother admonishes a daughter against anger, pride, jealousy, love of dress, &c., and is passionate herself, haughty, jealous, fond of dress, what must the daughter think but that the maxims of her mother are those of a mere actor, who is only playing a part? And when such an impression is made upon a child's mind in regard to parental inconsistency or insincerity, it is not easily removed, and is fatal to parental influence on all religious or moral subjects. On the other hand, a parent's silent but constant observance of all religious duties, and daily practice of Christian virtues and graces, "will take sure and gradual hold of the child's disposition, much beyond formal reproofs and chidings, which, being generally prompted by some present provocation, discover more of anger than of principle, and are always received with a temporary alienation and disgust." The first care, therefore of good parents is to be and practice themselves what they wish their children to be and practice.

9. Another method by which parents may best influence their children for good, is to make their religion amiable and their home attractive. Religion itself becomes offensive, especially to young minds, when it does not beam with cheerful kindness, but is coupled with forbidding manners, with moroseness, with rigorous severity, and intolerant exactions. True religion pulsates with joy and is radiant with smiles, and wins the heart of youth by

its loveliness, while it cheers the heart of age by its sweetness; but the croaking religion of "mint, anise, and cumin," alienates youth by its repulsiveness, and saddens age by its inexorableness. It is parsimonious in its liberalities, and miserly in its indulgences, and makes home a prison to children, instead of its being to them the happiest place on earth, where they can collect from time to time their chosen companions, feel the most freedom, and best enjoy their natural and innocent amusements, like the lambs of the sheepfold. If parents would protect their children from the snares and dangers of seeking social enjoyment abroad, they must make home the seat of such enjoyments. "For instance," as has been truly remarked, "if a father's economy degenerate into a minute and teasing parsimony, it is odd but that the son, who has suffered under it, sets out a sworn enemy to all rules of order and frugality. If a father's (or mother's) piety be morose, rigorous, and tinged with melancholy, perpetually breaking in upon the recreations of the family, and surfeiting them with the language of religion on all occasions, there is danger lest the son (or daughter) carry from home a settled prejudice against all seriousness and religion, as inconsistent with every plan of pleasurable life; and turn out, when mixing with the world, a character of levity, if not of dissoluteness." Another writer observes, with equal force, that "It is the duty of parents to strive to make home pleasant to their children. Children seldom fall into irregular and vicious habits when they have a happy home.

Parents should not allow the cares of life to render them silent, and perhaps morose, at home. They must not only love and labour for their children, they must sympathise with them. The great want of the young heart is sympathy. To their parents, above all others, have they a right to look for sympathy. If they do not find it at home, they will seek for it abroad."

10. But the duties of parents are not confined to the fireside, or limited to providing for the present physical, intellectual and moral wants of their children; they should endeavor to secure a trade or employment for their children, according to their habits and circumstances, and consistent with their best moral and religious interests; they should assist them, as far as possible, in their settlement in life; and while ceasing to exercise the authority of command, they should still continue to exercise over them the authority of counsel, of persuasion, of sympathy, of prayer; aiding their children, from time to time, according to exigencies and their own ability; and at death leaving to their families such provision as industry and economy, with the Divine blessing, may have enabled them to make, and according to the need and merits of each. But this should not be done in violation of scriptural commands and benevolence in behalf of the poor, and in support of Christian institutions. More children are ruined than benefited by inheriting, or settling in life with large fortunes. A shrewd observer has said, " The truth is, our children gain not so much as

we imagine, in the chance of this world's happiness, or even of its external prosperity, by setting out in life in it with large capital. Of those who have died rich, a great part began with little. And in respect of enjoyment, there is no comparison between a fortune which a man acquires by well applied industry, or by a series of successes in his business, and one found in his possession, or received from another."

LESSON V.

DUTY TO OUR NEIGHBOUR *(Continued)*: DUTY OF CHILDREN TO THEIR PARENTS.

21. *What is the first duty of Children to others?*— It is to love, reverence and obey their parents. The fifth commandment of God by Moses, and repeated by our Lord, and afterwards by the Apostle Paul, was, " Honour thy father and mother; which is the first commandment, with promise, that it may be well with thee, and that thou mayest live long on the earth " (Ex., 20: 12. Matt., 15: 4. Eph., 6: 2, 3).

22. *What do you understand by this duty to your Parents?*—I understand three things. *First*—I am to *love* my parents, as those to whom I am more indebted than to any other human beings; to whom I owe my existence, who fed me, clothed me, cared for me day and night when I could not talk, or walk, or help myself; who have often denied themselves of rest, and laboured much that they might

provide for me and educate me. *Secondly*—I am to *obey* my parents; that is, I am to do promptly and willingly whatever they direct me, without asking the why or wherefore of the command. *Thirdly*—I am to **honor,** or *reverence* my parents, which includes not only love and obedience, but that respect and deference which are due to those who are superior in age and wisdom, as well as in authority, and which I owe to my parents more than to any other persons.

23. *Do the Scriptures pronounce any punishment upon undutiful children?*—Yes; the punishment of death was commanded by God, under the Jewish law, to be inflicted upon "a stubborn and rebellious son, who will not obey the voice of his father or the voice of his mother, and that when they have chastised him, will not hearken to them," and especially when "he is a glutton and a drunkard" (Deut., 21: 18-21). In the 27th chapter of the same book, verse 16, are these terrible words: "Cursed is he that setteth light by his father or mother; and all the people shall say, Amen." In the 30th chapter of Proverbs, **verse 17, we** are told, "The eye that mocketh at his father and despiseth to obey his mother; the ravens of the valley shall pluck it out, and the young eagles shall eat it." This means, that he shall come to a violent death, and miserable end.

(NOTE.—The experience of all ages and countries testifies the fact, that disobedience to parents in youth is followed by disgrace and misfortune in manhood and old age.)

24. *How do the Scriptures commend (besides commanding) honour and obedience to parents?*—The Scriptures commend this duty as showing good qualities in a child. "A *wise son* heareth his father's instructions, but a *scorner* heareth not rebuke" (Prov., 13 : 1). They also commend it as a graceful ornament and adding beauty to the character of the child. "My son, keep the instruction of thy father, and forsake not the law of thy mother. They shall be an ornament of grace unto thy head, and chains about thy neck" (Prov., 1 : 8, 9). The Scriptures also pronounce a special blessing upon the dutiful child. The Apostle Paul says, that the commandment to honour thy father and mother, is the first, and indeed the only, comandment in the decalogue to which a special promise is attached;— "that it may be well with thee, and that thy days may be long in the land which the Lord thy God giveth thee" (Eph., 6 : 2, 3. Exodus, 20 : 12).

25. *But if a parent command a child to do wrong, is a child to obey?*—A child must obey God rather than man; as God is the highest parent, as well as the highest lawgiver. A child is not, therefore, to swear, to lie, to cheat, or to steal, even if a parent should be so unnatural and awfully wicked as to command it.

(NOTES ON THE DUTY OF CHILDREN TO PARENTS.—There are two painful cases in which children sometimes grossly disobey the command, "honour thy father and mother;"—the one case is that of treating their less educated father and mother with disrespect, and the other in not supporting them in old age when poor.

1. In the earliest settlement of this country the first born children had little or no opportunity of schools or of cultivated society. From their earliest years they had to employ all their time and strength to aid their immigrant parents to clear the land and provide the necessary food and clothing. But in the course of time, these first-born children of the country grew up, married, and by their industry and economy acquired a competency, so as to educate their children much better than they themselves had been educated. There is something more than great, there is something sublime, in the conduct of such parents, who, by pinching economy and untiring industry, have procured means and expended them in educating their children—perhaps sending their son to college and their daughter to a boarding school; but there is something more than mean, something inexpressibly contemptible and wicked, in that son and daughter treating such parents with neglect and disrespect because of their want of education and refinement. It is no dishonour, though a misfortune, for any persons, men or women, not to have had any opportunity or means of education in youth; but such persons are worthy of special attention and of double honour, especially from their children, if when they become parents, they deny themselves of many indulgences and comforts, and labour unceasingly, to confer upon their children educational advantages of which they, without any fault of their own, were deprived in early life. But for an educated daughter, thus educated, to flaunt contempt or disrespect upon such a mother because of her want of educational refinement, what a spectacle of ingratitude, meanness, and baseness of heart is it! And for an educated son, thus educated, to contemn, or treat with haughtiness, or disrespect, such an industrious and princely father, for his want of early education, what a spectacle of heartless ingratitude and moral degradation is it! Better and more honorable to be the uneducated, but large-hearted and noble father and mother in such a case, than to be the ungrateful and despicable educated son or daughter.

But parents who have means to educate their children, and deny to their children the education which other parents in like circumstances provide for their children, or parents who set a profligate or vicious example before their children, have only themselves to blame if they receive not from their children due respect and honour. Yet children thus neglected, or hardly treated, or badly taught, are not thereby exempted from the duty of honoring and obeying their parents. Though the conduct of a parent may cancel the obligations of gratitude, other obligations remain.

2. A second case of ungratefulness requiring special remark, is that of a son refusing or neglecting to support his aged and indigent parents. The teaching of our Lord on this subject is evinced by the indignation with which he denounced the wretched casuistry of the Pharisees, (Mark, 7: 10-13), who contrived, by pretending to convert so much of their property to the service of the temple, to evade this duty of children to their father and mother. "Agreeably to this law of Nature and Christianity (says Paley), children are, by the law of England, bound to support, as well their immediate parents, as their grandfather and grandmother, or remoter ancestors, who stand in need of support." Dr. Wayland remarks, "That man is guilty of monstrous ingratitude, who would not cheerfully deny himself of luxuries or conveniences, in order to minister to the wants of his aged and needy parents." Another writer justly and touchingly observes, "Time, in its never-ceasing progress, reverses the order in which life began; the child becomes a parent, and the parent by-and-by becomes again a child. The arms that held us in infancy, require now the strength of our more robust and vigorous forms; the hands that toiled and the feet that moved so readily for all our wants, must now depend upon us for support. By every little act of kindness and attention, by all the sweet and soothing ministry of love, it is for us to discharge that debt. Happy for us, if over the grave of a parent, we never have occasion to drop a tear of regret, that we were, in any measure, negligent of this sacred duty.")

CHRISTIAN MORALS.

LESSON VI.

DUTY TO OUR NEIGHBOUR *(Continued);* DUTY OF CHILDREN AND YOUNG PEOPLE TO EACH OTHER AND TO OLD PEOPLE.

52. *What is your second duty to others, or your first duty after that which you owe to your parents?*—My first duty to others, next to that which I owe to my parents, is that which I owe to my brothers and sisters; never to provoke them, or call them ill names, or make sport of them, or take what belongs to them, or do anything to make them unhappy; but always to show that I love and respect them, that I will help them when necessary, be obliging to them, and do all I can to make them happy, and to make them respect and love me.

26. *What is your third duty to others?*—My third duty to others is that which I owe to my school fellows and other children and young people—to do to them in all things, and at all times, what I would wish them to do to me in like circumstances; that as I would not wish to be treated with disrespect or unkindly, to be tattled about, to be called ill names, to be vexed, or be deprived of what belongs to me, so I should do nothing of the kind in regard to others, but try to oblige every one and to make every one as happy as possible.

27. *What is your duty to old people?*—I should treat them with more than ordinary respect; I should treat them with affectionate reverence—offer them my seat at church, or in any public meeting, or other place, if I had one and they had none, and

2*

do all in my power to promote their convenience and comfort.

(NOTE ON THE **DUTY OF** CHILDREN AND YOUNG PERSONS TO THE AGED.—God said by Moses, nearly fifteen hundred years before Christ, "Thou shalt rise **up** before the hoary head, and honour the **face of** the old man" (Lev. 19: 32). Herodotus, who wrote his history a thousand years **after** Moses, says, "If a young person meet his senior he instantly turns aside to make way for him; if an aged person enter an apartment, the youth **always rise from** their seats" (Euterpe, c. 80). Among the characteristics of the degeneracy of the Jewish people, and the causes of their national **ruin,** was disrespect of age. Isaiah mentions the "child **behaving** himself proudly against the ancient" (Is. **3**: 5); and Jeremiah says, "the faces **of the** elders were not honoured" (Lam. 5: 12). Among the ancient Romans, **not to** rise up in the presence of an aged person was **deemed not** only **an awful mark** of deep degeneracy, but **was** considered a crime worthy of death. Thus Juvenal says—

> "Credebant quo grande nefas, et morte piandum,
> Si juvenis vetulo non assurexerat; et si
> Barbato cuicumque puer," &c.—(Sat. 13, v. 54).

Lines which have been translated by Gifford, thus:

> "It was a crime
> Worthy of death, such awe did years [inspire],
> If manhood rose not up to reverend age,
> And youth to manhood."

In England respect is still paid to age, in the State, in **the** Church, and in the social circle; but among the signs of the times and ill omens for America, **is** the lamentable absence of respect for **age** on the **part of the** younger generation—so manifest not only in civil **affairs,** but in ecclesiastical assemblies and in all the **social** intercourse of life. Old people are often jostled, and **sometimes** even jeered, instead of being reverenced and treated as **the** fathers of the land. It becomes **every** youth in Canada, and every friend of the civilization and future welfare of our country, to obey the Divine command, and imitate the noble examples, not only of the Scriptures, but of ancient heathen nations, to honour old age, and avoid and discountenance the unnatural and portentous degeneracy of treating aged people with disrespect or indifference.

Note on the duty of children and young people to each other.—Nothing contributes more to the happiness of a family, and its credit in the neighbourhood, than mutual respect and affection among brothers and sisters, accompanied with, as it almost invariably is, and resulting therefrom, honour and obedience to parents, and a due respect and attention on the part of parents to children; and one of the essential and most potent elements of the happiness and elevation of a neighbourhood is the mutual deportment of respect and kindness among its youth and young people towards each other.)

LESSON VII.

DUTIES TO ONE'S SELF; SELF-CONTROL.

27. *What is your first duty to yourself?*—My first duty to myself is to control myself.

28. *What do you mean by controlling yourself?*— By controlling myself I mean, that I must govern my temper, appetites, passions and propensities.

29. *Why should you govern your temper?*—I should govern my temper for four reasons. *First*—Because I wish to be free, and act at all times under the control of reason, judgment and principle, and not be under the tyranny of a passion, which is a sort of madness, lawless and ungovernable, the sport of events, acting without reason, and often against reason; and, like St. Vitus' dance, controlling its

victim when and however the fits take him. *Second*—Because I do not wish to be the slave of any one who may wish to provoke me, for his own purpose, and to make himself merry at my expense. *Third*—Because I wish to respect myself, and one cannot yield to every breath of angry passion without losing self-respect. *Fourth*—Because I wish to obey the commands and imitate the example of my Saviour, who is altogether lovely, and obtain a greatness within my reach, which exceeds that of heroes or conquerors; for the Scripture has said, " He that is slow to anger, is better than the mighty; and he that ruleth his spirit, than he that taketh a city." (Prov. 16: 32).

30. *What do you mean by passions, appetites and propensities?*—By passions I mean violent agitations or excitements of the mind; by appetites, I mean strong desires for food or drink, or anything sensual; by propensities, I mean strong tendencies or bent of the mind to particular objects—especially to objects of the senses.

31. *Why should you govern your passions, appetites and propensities?*—I should govern my passions, appetites and propensities, because they should be my servants and not my masters—useful when directed to proper objects and in a proper manner, but hurtful and destructive when indulged without control, and until they become one's tormentors and then one's destroyers.

(NOTES ON THE DUTY OF SELF-CONTROL.—1. *Anger.*—An irritable, discontented and quarrelsome person is not only a cause of discomfort to others, but can never be happy himself. Such an one, whether boy or girl, whether man or woman, and in whatever outward circumstances, carries within the bosom what embitters life. The excitement of anger renders clear perception and sound judgment impossible. An angry person sees everything through a distorted medium, and utters words and commits acts which afterwards appear foolish and unjust even to their author. It is true, the Bible says, "Be ye angry and sin not" (Eph. 4: 26); thereby indicating that there is a kind of anger which is not sinful. Thus God is said to be angry with the wicked every day; but by this is meant his holy indignation against wrong-doing; and God has given us such a moral constitution, that we cannot witness acts of injustice and cruelty without a feeling of indignation. But this right feeling is very different from anger in its ordinary acceptation, which is a perversion of that capacity of our nature—that feeling of disapprobation and indignation which wrong-doing excites within us.

The Scripture says, "Charity (or love) suffereth long, is not easily provoked." "Let every man be slow to wrath," and "let not the sun go down upon your wrath." "Let all anger be put away."

These precepts of Scripture, as well as all reasoning on the subject, imply that the passion of anger is under our control. Persons do, indeed, greatly differ in their natural tempers. Some are calm, and not easily excited to anger, while others are very susceptible of angry feeling. But that the outbursts and all the sinful feelings of anger may in all cases be controlled, is obvious, not only from what is implied and enjoined in the Scriptures, but also from the fact that the most fretful and impatient persons, who harrass their families and juniors with their peevish and intemperate sallies, are able to restrain their ebullitions of anger in the presence of superiors, or in regard to equals who would chastise them for outrageous conduct.

Yet when anger is the "easily besetting sin" of a person, however young or old, it is an enemy not to be easily, if at all, subdued and kept in subjection, without prayer to the Source of all meekness as well as of all strength; but there are certain instrumentalities or helps for the subjection of a passion so destructive of both personal happiness and influence. One is an ever-cultivated consciousness of the Divine presence, and of our imperfections before and in respect to Him; another is silence, the means adopted by Socrates, whenever he felt the passion rising in his mind, by which he avoided many occasions of giving offence to others, and thus extinguished in the seed this great bane of human happiness. And next to silence, "a soft answer turneth away wrath," not only in the hearer, but also, and especially, in the speaker, and exhibits more heroic and noble courage than the most vehement invectives of anger.

2. *Passions, Appetites, Propensities.*—The control of the temper is one of the noblest of conquests, and the more so when it is maintained under a sense of insult or injury received; but self-control relates not only to the temper, but involves due restraint of all our passions, appetites and propensities. This is what is meant by *temperance*—the avoidance of all those excesses which impair the strength and activity of body and mind, injure the health, destroy character and influence, often cut short life itself—consequences and results which, sooner or later, as surely follow the unrestrained indulgence of the passions and appetites of our animal nature, as that effect follows cause, or night succeeds day; and they should therefore be guarded against with more vigilance than defence against the robber and the assassin. The lawless indulgence of the passions and appetites involves, in some cases, *sensuality;* and sensuality ruins both body and mind. "He who yields to this foe is lost." Such indulgence, in other cases, involves **drunkenness;** and the mischief of drunkenness is thus summed up by Paley: "1. It betrays most constitutions either to **extravagances** of anger or sins of lewdness. 2. It disqualifies men for the duties of their station,

both by the temporary disorders of their faculties, and at length by incapacity and stupefaction. 3. It is attended with expenses, which can often ill be spared. 4. It is sure to occasion uneasiness to the family of the drunkard. 5. It shortens life."

But in all cases the loss of self-control over the temper and various animal propensities of our nature, involves the loss of self-respect; and that is a loss which gold cannot repay, and is destructive of character. It also involves the inevitable loss of the respect of others. "No man can, for any length of time, receive the real homage and respect of others, who lacks the mastery of himself. Station, power, wealth, may do something for him; native talent and genius, still more; but not even these can ultimately keep back from merited contempt the helpless slave of his own miserable passions. Sad indeed is the spectacle, of one born to high honors, and endowed by nature with princely gifts, from whose hand is stricken the sceptre of dominion over his own spirit."

The only effectual remedy (even as a matter of prudence, apart from Divine aid) against any bad habit of temper, or animal passion or appetite, which may have been contracted, or to which one is liable, is a rigid rule of action. "I own myself (says Paley) a friend to the laying down rules to ourselves of this sort, and rigidly abiding by them. They may be exclaimed against as stiff, but they are often salutary. Indefinite resolutions of abstemiousness are apt to yield to *extraordinary* occasions; and *extraordinary* occasions are apt to occur perpetually. Whereas, the stricter the rule is, the more tenacious we grow of it; and many a man will abstain rather than break his rule, who would not easily be brought to exercise the same mortification from higher motives: not to mention, that when our rule is once known, we are provided with an answer to every importunity.")

LESSON VIII.

DUTY TO SELF; CULTURE OF THE MIND.

32. *After controlling your temper, passions and appetites, what is the next duty which you owe to yourself?*—My next duty is to improve my mind.

33. *Why should you improve your mind?*—I should improve my mind because it is the noblest part of me—it is my very self: for without the mind, the rest of me is earth—an earthly house which is to be dissolved (2 Cor. 5: 1); and it is my duty, as well as my interest, to cultivate that nature which I have in common with the angels and with God. Self-culture, no less than self-control, is a duty which I owe to myself, to my family, to society at large, and to my Creator.

34. *What do you mean by improving your mind?*—By improving my mind, I mean developing it, or making it grow strong by active labour; for as the arm, or any member of the body, or the body itself, grows strong by exercise, so is it with the powers of the mind. Activity and industrious application strengthen it and make it manly, while idleness and sloth make it weak, cowardly and unstable.

35. *How should you improve your mind?*—I should do several things. *First*, I should do all in my power to read well, to write well, and to do arithmetic well, and to understand and write and speak my native language well. *Second*, I should learn something of myself—how fearfully and wonderfully

I am made in both body and mind; nor should I remain in ignorance of the nature and laws of God's works above, and around, and beneath me, and how they are to be employed for the good of man. I should especially learn the why and the wherefore of each kind of work I have to do, whether in the mechanic's shop, in the manufactory, or on the farm; so as not to work as a mere tool, or an ox or a horse, but as an intelligent actor, in harmony with the laws which God has impressed upon his works for the study, and practice, and welfare of man. *Third,* I should know something of the surface of the globe on which I live, and therefore study its geography; I should know something of the people who have lived at different times in various parts the world, their laws, and customs, and doings, and therefore study history; I ought to know something of the great men who have written for the instruction, or have influenced the affairs of mankind, and should therefore read their biography and study their works, as far as I may be able. *Fourth,* I should listen to and seek the conversation of those who know more than myself, and especially on subjects with which they may be professionally or respectively well acquainted. *Fifth,* I should carefully *observe* the objects and occurrences of every-day life, whether sensible or intellectual—whether relating to persons or things. *Sixth,* I should improve, by study and meditation, the hints I have received from reading, conversation, and observation. *Seventh,* I should humbly and believingly pray the Author of Mind to teach my mind, and to bless my efforts to improve, to strengthen, and to enlarge it.

(NOTES ON SELF-CULTURE AND MENTAL IMPROVEMENT.—It is not within the scope of these *First Lessons* to treat of the higher subjects of Mathematics or Metaphysics, the study of which is usually commended as instruments of mental discipline and power, though I am inclined to think, with Dr. Watts, that the study of history and of the principles of the Divine and of human governments, as well as of natural science, are not less so, and are more practical. These, at least, have been the subjects of my own studies since early life.

2. Proper self-culture includes the body as well as the mind —careful physical as well as mental training; for a well-developed and healthy physical organism is one of the choicest blessings of life. A sound mind in a sound body is a maxim both of philosophy and morals which should never be forgotten; and care and effort should be employed for the development and discipline of our physical, no less than of our mental faculties.

3. Nor should it be forgotten that the improvement of the physical, intellectual and moral powers is a *duty* of every man, and a duty embracing manhood as well as youth—a duty which cannot be neglected without heinous ingratitude and guilt. God has not endowed man with such capacities of improvement, activity and usefulness, to be dwarfed by neglect, any more than to be degraded by vicious indulgence. And it should be remembered that the growth of mind is not limited to youth, but is susceptible of the largest developments after the body has attained its maturity. A man should be a student all his life, and not, as is too often the case, lay aside his mental discipline and culture as soon as he commences professional or business pursuits. Just as a man's professional or other business begins to decline as soon as he begins to neglect it; so he begins to decline in his mental powers and tastes as

soon as he begins to neglect their improvement. No man has a right so to engage in the pursuits of business as to give no time and care to the improvement of his mind. He who made mind, with its wondrous faculties, had no such design; and man should not rob God, any more than himself, by either the neglect or the abuse of the Divine endowments.

4. Nor should mental culture be pursued merely as a means of success in the employments of life. Such a means it undoubtedly is; but aside from that, and far above it, power and wealth of mind is a good in itself. And by this culture I mean not only the intellect, strictly speaking, but the memory, the judgment, the reasoning powers, the imagination, the taste, the conscience, the will, the heart—man's whole moral and sensitive, as well as intellectual nature. No material wealth can compare with the treasures of an enriched and well cultivated mind; not like other riches which are external, often accompanied by the mental disquietude and wretchedness of the occupant, and often taking wings of flight, but a part of the soul itself, and remaining an inalienable inheritance while the mind itself has being. "Wisdom is better than rubies; and all the things that may be desired are not to be compared to it" (Prov., 8: 11).

5. It is also to be observed, that such mental culture does not so much depend on outward, or even early advantages, as upon individual determination and industry. Some of the brightest names in the history of religion, science and literature, are those who, in early years, were children of poverty and toil, and who, in after years, were pressed by the duties of active life. Industry, perseverence, judicious method, with the Divine blessing, will conquer all difficulties, and achieve success in the most adverse circumstances.)

LESSON IX.

SELF-CONSECRATION.

36. *What other duties do you owe to yourself besides those of self-control and self-culture?*—I owe to myself the duty of self-consecration and veracity.

37. *What do you mean by self-consecration?*—By self-consecration, I mean that I should be a Christian—that this should be my first aim, my first care and first effort.

38. *Why should you make self-consecration your chief duty to yourself?*—I should make self-consecration the chief duty to myself for several reasons: *First*—My safety depends upon it. It is only when God "holdeth me up that I am safe," (Psalm 119: 117); otherwise I am exposed to every snare and danger without protection. *Second*—My happiness depends upon it; for God is the only source of happiness; and without his favour and friendship no one can be truly happy. *Third*—My interests depend upon it; for the "blessing of the Lord, it maketh rich, and he addeth no sorrow thereto," (Prov., 10: 22); and to consecrate to God the morning of my life, is to secure his blessing throughout the whole of life's day. "Godliness is profitable unto all things, having the promise of the life that now is, and of that which is to come," (1 Timothy, 4: 8).

39. *What is required by your self-consecration?*—It is required that I should use the means of grace

which God has appointed for that **purpose**; of which are the sacraments, namely, baptism and **the Lord's supper**; that if I have not been baptized, I should apply to be baptized; that if I have been baptized, I should fulfil the obligations of my baptism.

40. *What do you* **mean** *by the word* *sacrament?*—"I mean by the word sacrament **an** outward and visible sign **of an** inward and spiritual grace, given unto us, **ordained** by Christ himself, as a means whereby we receive the same, and **a** pledge to assure us thereof."

41. *What is the outward and visible* **sign or form** *of baptism?*—The outward and visible sign or form in baptism is the application of water in the name of the Father, **and of** the **Son, and of** the Holy Ghost, (Matthew, 28: 19).

42. *What is the inward and spiritual grace signified by this?*—The inward and spiritual grace signified by baptism is, our being cleansed **from sin, and** becoming new creatures in Christ Jesus (Acts 22: 16).

43. *What are the actual privileges of baptized persons?*—The actual privileges of baptized persons are these; they are made members of the visible church of Christ; their gracious relation to Him as the Second Adam, **and as the** Mediator **of the New Covenant, is** solemnly ratified by Divine appointment; and they are thereby recognized as having a claim to all those spiritual blessings, **of which they** are the proper subjects.

44. *What does your baptism in the name of the Father, the Son, and the Holy Ghost oblige you to do?* —My baptism in the name of the Father, the Son, and the Holy Ghost, obliges me, first, to renounce the devil and all his works, the pomps and vanity of this wicked world, and all the sinful lusts of the flesh; secondly, that I should believe all the articles of the Christian faith; and, thirdly, that I should keep God's holy will and commandments, and walk in the same all the days of my life.

45. *Why was the sacrament of the Lord's Supper ordained?*—The sacrament of the Lord's supper was ordained for the continual remembrance of the sacrifice of the death of Christ, and of the benefits we receive thereby (1 Cor. 11: 23-26).

46. *What is the outward part or sign of the Lord's Supper?*—The outward part or sign of the Lord's Supper is bread and wine, which the Lord hath commanded to be received (Matthew, 26: 26-28).

47. *What is the thing signified by this outward sign?*—The thing signified by the outward sign of bread and wine in the Lord's Supper, is the body and blood of Christ, which are spiritually taken and received by the faithful in the Lord's Supper, to the strengthening and refreshing of their souls (1 Cor., 10: 16; John, 6: 54, 55).

48. *Why ought you to partake of the Lord's Supper regularly and frequently?*—I ought to partake of the Lord's Supper regularly and frequently, first, in

obedience to Christ's commandment, "This do in remembrance of me" (Luke, 22: 19); secondly, **to make a holy profession of Christ** and his cross, **by declaring** my entire dependence on his death as the only atonement **for our sins**, and as the only **hope** of salvation; thirdly, to declare my love and thankfulness to him, and **to enjoy** communion with God, and with our fellow-Christians, in the remembrance of Christ's death.

49. *What is required of you in coming to the Lord's Supper?*—It is required of me, in coming to the Lord's Supper, to examine myself, whether I repent myself truly of my former sins, steadfastly purposing to lead a holy life; and whether I have a lively **faith** in **God's** mercy through Christ, with a thankful remembrance of his death, and am in charity **with all men.** (1 Cor. 11: 28.)

LESSON X.

VERACITY.

50. *What do you mean by veracity?*—By veracity I mean habitual observance of truth in all my words and conduct; it is the opposite **of a lie or** falsehood, which is the utterance of an untruth **with intention** to deceive.

51. *How may truth or falsehood be uttered?*—**Truth or falsehood** may be uttered by words, by gestures, **by looks,** and sometimes by silence; the essence of the truth or falsehood being, not in the words employed, but in the impression intended to be made.

52. *Why do you owe it to yourself always to speak the truth?*—I owe it to myself always to speak the truth for the following reasons: *First*—My own safety and salvation are involved in it. The Scriptures everywhere command to speak the truth and lie not. "Lying lips are an abomination unto the Lord; but they that deal truly are his delight" (Prov. 12: 22). "Wherefore, putting away lying, speak every man truth with his neighbour" (Eph. 4: 25). "All liars shall have their part in the lake which burneth with fire and brimstone; which is the second death" (Rev. 21: 8). *Secondly*—Self-respect requires me always to speak the truth; for I could not lie, any more than I could steal, without losing all respect for myself; and the loss of self-respect leads to ruin. *Thirdly*—My reputation and character requires me always to speak the truth. No one is more respected than one who is never known to swerve from the truth, while all agree that lying is the meanest of vices, and a liar is shunned and despised by everybody. *Fourthly*—In my relations to society, as a citizen, I am bound to speak the truth. A lie is an insult of the grossest nature to him to whom it is uttered; it destroys confidence between man and man, and thus strikes at the very foundations of society.

(NOTES ON LYING.—Paley remarks, "A lie is a breach of promise; for whoever seriously addresses his discourse to another, tacitly promises to speak the truth, because he knows that truth is expected." But it does not follow that all untrue statements are lies. A person may make untrue statements, believing them to be true. It is the *intention to deceive*—the deception—which is the essential element of a lie. Thus, a statement literally or verbally true, yet may be a lie in the sense in which the hearer or reader would be likely to understand it, and in which sense the speaker or writer intended to be understood. On the other hand, statements may be made which are not true in themselves, but where there is no intention to deceive, and no one is deceived. Such are parables, fictions, dramas, allegories, &c. The medium of fiction is employed for amusement or instruction, without any understanding on the part of the author or reader, the speaker or hearer, that the story is an exact narration of facts. Thus fiction may convey truth in the most impressive way; and parables are fictitious narratives employed to communicate truth.

2. There is one species of lying not uncommon, but not the less to be avoided and condemned. Some persons, in order to render their conversation spicy and amusing, and without, perhaps, intending to depart from truth, exaggerate and colour their statements, so that it is difficult to distinguish between the true and the false. Such persons may not be regarded as deceivers; but they are likely to lose the confidence of their acquaintances; their statements cannot be relied upon or safely repeated. Paley says: "I have seldom known any one who deserted truth in trifles, that could be trusted in matters of importance. Nice distinctions are out of the question, upon occasions which, like those of speech, return every hour. The habit, therefore, of lying, when once formed, is easily extended to serve the designs of malice or interest: like all habits, it spreads indeed of itself." Dr. Wayland forcibly remarks: "There is no vice which, more easily than this, stupifies a man's conscience. He who tells lies frequently will soon become an habitual liar, and an habitual liar will soon lose the power of distinguishing between the conceptions of his imagi

nation and the recollections of his memory. I have known a few persons who seemed to have arrived at this most deplorable moral condition. Let every one, therefore, beware of even the most distant approaches to this detestable vice."

3. I may add, that truth is too sacred to be trifled with on any occasion or for any purpose. It is as much our duty to speak the truth at all times as it is to be honest at all times, and in small as well as great matters. "He that is unfaithful in that which is least, is unfaithful also in much; and he that is unjust in the least, is unjust also in much" (Luke, 16: 10).

NOTE.—I enter not here into the questions of casuistry—so largely discussed in some books—as to whether there can be any justification for professional or political lying, or lying to save life in case of encountering a robber, or a madman. This much may be safely said: there can be no morality, and therefore no principle, in any political or professional proceeding, in which lying is a necessity, or what is unjust between man and man, expedient.)

LESSON XI.

RIGHT AND WRONG—CONSCIENCE.

53. In the preceding Lessons some actions have been commended as right and other actions have been condemned as wrong; *Can you tell on what the distinction between right and wrong is founded?* I think the distinction of right and wrong is founded in the eternal and immutable nature of things, and is eternal and immutable as God himself. It is before all law, and is the origin of all law.

54. *Have we any proof in ourselves of this distinction between right and wrong actions?*—Yes; "every

one knows that he perceives certain actions to be right or wrong. Every one feels that it is wrong to lie, to steal, to murder, to be cruel. Every one feels that it is right to tell the truth, to be honest, affectionate, kind and grateful. If any one do wrong, as, for instance, if he lie, or steal, or abuse another person, he feels a peculiar sort of unhappiness, which is called the feeling of guilt; he is afraid of being detected, he wishes he had not done it, and if he be detected, he knows that every one dislikes and despises his conduct. And, on the other hand, if he have done right, as, if he have told the truth, have been grateful, or have returned good for evil, he feels a peculiar sort of pleasure, he is satisfied with himself, and knows that all men will look upon him with respect."

55. *Wherein does* **this moral** *quality* **of** *human actions consist?*—This moral quality of human actions consists in the *intention*. A good intention is necessary to a good action; a bad **intention is necessary to** a bad action. It is the *intention* which determines the moral character of actions.

56. *What* **is that capacity or** *power within us called which discerns* **and pronounces upon** *the moral quality of actions?*—That capacity or **power which** discerns and pronounces within us upon the moral quality of actions, is called conscience, or the moral **sense.**

57. *What proof* **have we** *of the existence* **of** *conscience?*—We have the same proof of the existence of conscience that we have of any other faculty or

power of the mind. "The faculty of the understanding (says Reid), is capable of knowledge; the faculty of the judgment compares; the faculty of the will chooses and refuses; the faculty of the conscience distinguishes right and wrong, and approves and disapproves of our actions."

(NOTES ON THE LESSON.—1. *Perceptions of right and wrong—Truth and error.*—The idea of right and wrong is among the first principles of the human mind; requires and admits of no definition; manifests itself with the dawn of reason; is common alike to the simple and the learned, the child and the philosopher. There may be differences of opinion as to what is and what is not right action; the teaching of one system and of one age may pronounce right acts which the teaching of another system and of another age may pronounce wrong; but every system and every age admits and assumes the essential difference between right and wrong. Every person who knows there is a difference between white and black, knows there is a difference between right and wrong; he knows that he ought to do right, and that he ought not to do wrong. He knows that this is his duty, though he may not always know what his duty is, or always do it when he does know it. If it be asked how we know the difference between right and wrong, how we know some things are true and some things are false, the answer is, we cannot tell; the mind sees them to be so, just as it sees the whole is greater than a part, that the shortest distance between two points is a straight line, that two and two make four. These self-evident propositions are called intuitive truths; and the mind directly or intuitively perceives them as soon as stated. But in what their truth consists, and how the mind perceives it, admits of no answer. So the mind intuitively perceives some actions to be right, and other actions to be wrong,—such as one man rescuing another from drowning, or restoring money entrusted to him for safe-keeping, or one man drowning another, or stealing the money of another; **but how or why we see the one act right and the other wrong, no answer can be given.** If it be said one is an act of benevolence and justice, and the other an act of cruelty **and** dishonesty, it may be asked, why **so?** If it be **answered,** again, **the one tends to** promote happiness, **and** the **other to** cause misery, **the reply is, why is it** right to promote happiness, and wrong **to cause misery?** We are shut up to the answer, because **the one is right and the other wrong.**

I make these remarks and adduce **these** illustrations to show the absurdity **of** some persons pretending to doubt or object to certain things which cannot be proved, being subjects of consciousness, **or objects** of direct perception.

But while some **truths, as in** the **above examples, are intuitively** perceived, **other truths are arrived at by a process of reasoning,**—such as **the existence of an author and** printer by seeing a book. Often the truth of a proposition depends upon **the truth of several** other propositions, **the truth** of each of **which** must be known **before** the truth **of the** first proposition can be known,—such as many propositions in geometry, and many truths in politics, agriculture, commerce, &c.

So also, while some acts **are intuitively perceived to be right** or wrong, the perception of the **rightness or** wrongness of other acts may depend upon our perception of many other things connected with them. In all our reasonings in regard to either duty or **doctrine,** the human mind is liable to err, as it is not infallible; **but of intuitive** truths we are as certain as we are **of our existence, or that we see an** object or hear a sound.

2. Remarks on Conscience.—Opinions **differ as to** whether conscience is a **faculty** of the mind, **or a** function of the mind, **or the** mind itself acting **on** moral questions, or **the moral nature of man.** The late Dr. Alexander, of Edinburgh, **in the** Encyclopædia Britannica, says—"The moral **nature of man is summed up** in the **word** conscience. **Moral nature and conscience are two** names of the same **thing. The analysis of**

conscience, therefore, will **unfold man's** moral nature." Dr. Wayland, in his Moral Science, says, "Conscience is that faculty of the mind by which we distinguish between right and wrong in our actions, whether they have respect to our fellow men or to God." Dr. Alden, in his Christian Ethics, says, "**Conscience is** defined to be the **power** by which the mind perceives **the** difference between right and wrong. But the **power of the** mind is not **something** separate from the mind. When **we** speak of the **mind** having certain powers **or** faculties, we mean that the mind **can do** certain things. **When** the mind **perceives** external **objects**, through the agency **of the** senses, it is said to be **exercising the** faculty of perception. When the mind **recalls past events, it** is said to be exercising the faculty of memory. **When** the mind perceives truths, **by means** of other truths, **it is said to be** exercising the reasoning faculty. When the mind perceives duty, it is said **to be exercising the moral faculty, or** conscience. The expressions, '**conscience makes us know our duty,**' and '**the mind perceives duty,**' **have the same** meaning. The **first** form of expression is figurative, **the** second is literal. **We are** much less liable to error, **when we** use literal, than when we **use** figurative expressions. When it is said that **conscience is an original attribute of our nature, the meaning is, that the human** mind **was made with the power of perceiving right** and **wrong.** When **it is** said **that conscience is fallible, the** meaning is, the **mind may make mistakes as to** duty." Dr. M. Hopkins, in his Lectures on Moral Science, remarks—"By many, by most, conscience is regarded as a separate faculty, and, **as has been said, the whole** of our moral nature. I prefer to say, **that** it is **a function of** moral reason. **It may be** defined **as** that function of moral reason by which **it affirms** obligation before the act, **by which** it approves **or** disapproves **after the act,** and by which it indicates future **reward** or punishment. Conscience will then reveal itself as, 1st. Obligatory. 2nd. Judicial. 3rd. Prophetic. These **will** be, first, the affirmation of obligation before the act; second, the excusing or accusing **by one** another of the thoughts after the **act: and,** third, a promise or threat that becomes, on the one hand, a hope of eternal life, or, on the other, 'a certain fearful looking for of judgment.'"

But whatever may be the diversity of terms or of expression, all agree as to the existence and office of conscience. Of its tremendous and often crushing power we have frequent illustrations. It has compelled the disclosure of crimes which no other human searching could discover, and has been more terrible in its inflictions than the penalties of any human laws. Its approval inspires courage as well as imparts satisfaction; its disapproval excites fear, and inflicts pain—illustrating both the philosophy and truth of the Scripture apothegm, "The righteous is as bold as a lion; the wicked fleeth when no man pursueth." Dr. Wayland truly remarks—"This is one great reason why persons who have done wrong are so fearful and cowardly; and why those who have done well are so much bolder. He who has done wrong knows that he deserves to be punished; and hence he is afraid that every body is going to punish him. He who has done well, knows that he deserves to be rewarded, and hence he is afraid of no one. And this is one reason why those who have done wrong are so commonly found out. He who has done wrong is afraid and ashamed, he shows it in his countenance and actions; and the more he tries to conceal it, the more clearly he discovers it. Thus the Bible tells us that the wicked is snared in the work of his own hands; and though hand join in hand, the wicked shall not go unpunished." Dr. Joseph Haven, in his Moral Philosophy, remarks with much force upon this subject: "Herein lies the power of an approving or accusing conscience. The proposition now stands, 'I have done well,' 'I have done ill;' and in that simple verdict, calmly rendered, but seldom reversed, lies a sustaining or condemning power, greater than that of thrones and armies—a power that can look danger in the face, and defy a world in arms—a power that can make the guilty man tremble, though surrounded by all that wealth, and station, and princely dignity can confer."

It is also to be observed, that while conscience is an original faculty of the mind, and its authority more or less felt in every situation, it may be darkened and debased by ignorance and vice, as well as enlightened by moral and religious culture. God, who has endowed us with our moral powers, has entrusted to us and imposed upon us the duty of cultivating them by heeding their admonitions and acquainting ourselves with our duty, as he has also required of us the culture of our intellectual and physical powers by appropriate studies and exercises. Even in respect to the heathen, the inspired Apostle says, "For when the Gentiles, which have not the law, do by nature the things contained in the law, these, having not the law, are a law unto themselves; which show the work of the law written in their hearts, their *conscience* also bearing witness, and their thoughts the meanwhile accusing or else excusing one another" (Rom. 2: 14, 15). On these words Dr. Dewar, in his Moral Philosophy, justly remarks: "The argument is this: the Gentiles, who had not the law by revelation, showed that its substance was engraven on their hearts by the influence which conscience exercised over them. That power, though darkened and weakened by sin, remonstrated with them when they did wrong, and encouraged and approved of them when they did right. Their own conceptions of right and wrong, under its influence and authority, formed the rule of their conduct; and in proportion as they approached this standard or deviated from it, did they feel self-approbation or self-reproach; their thoughts accused or else excused one another. They thus had the testimony in themselves, and gave evidence to others, that they were the subjects of moral law and government, and accountable for their conduct to the Supreme Lord and Ruler of all."

The practical lesson is, the reader should ask himself, in regard to every pursuit, and association, and act, *what is right*, and do it because it is right, as also for the sake of both safety and happiness.

3. REMARKS ON THE DIFFERENT THEORIES OF MORAL VIRTUE, AND THE GROUNDS OF MORAL OBLIGATION.—From the various

theories which ancient and modern philosophers and moralists have advocated as to the essence of moral virtue and the ground of moral obligation, the inexperienced reader is liable to suppose that there must be some uncertainty in the one or the other, or in both; whereas this very diversity is only a *cumulative* testimony to the beauty and excellence of moral virtue, and the reality and strength of moral obligation. This subject is beautifully elucidated by the following remarks of the eloquent Dr. Chalmers, in his Natural Theology:

"Each partizan has advocated his own theory; and each, in doing so, has more fully exhibited some distinct property or perfection of moral rectitude. Morality is not destroyed by this conflict of testimonies, but rises in statelier pride and with augmented security from the foam and the turbulence which play around its base. For when it is asserted by one party in the strife, that 'the foundation of morality is the right of God to the obedience of his creatures,' let God's absolute right be fully conceded to them. And when others reply, that, 'apart from such right, there is a native and essential rightness in morality,' let this be conceded also. There is indeed such a rightness, which, anterior to law, has had everlasting residence in the character of the Godhead, and which prompted Him to a law whose enactments bear the impress of purest morality.

"And when advocates of the selfish system affirm that 'the good of self is the sole aim and principle of virtue,' while we refuse their theory, let us at least admit the fact to which all its plausibility is owing, that naught conduces more to happiness than the strict observance of all the recognized moralities of human conduct.

"And when a fourth party affirms that 'naught but the useful is virtuous,' and, in support of their theory, can state the unvarying tendencies of virtue in the world toward the highest good of the human family, let it be forthwith granted, that the same God who blends in his own person both the rightness of morality and the right of law, has so devised the economy of things, and so directs his processes, as to make peace and prosperity follow in the train of righteousness.

"And when the position that 'virtue is its own reward,' is cast as another dogma into the whirlpool of debate, let it be fondly allowed, that the God who delights in moral excellence himself, has made it the direct minister of enjoyment to him who, formed after his own image, delights in it also. And when others, expatiating on the 'beauty of virtue,' would almost rank it among the objects of taste rather than of principle, let this be followed up by the kindred testimony that, in all its exhibitions there is indeed a supreme gracefulness; and that God, rich and varied in all the attestations which he has given of his regard to it, has also so endowed his creatures, that, in moral worth, they have the beatitudes of taste as well as the beatitudes of conscience.

"And should there be philosophers who say of morality that 'it is wholly founded upon the emotions,' let it at least be granted, that He whose hand did frame our internal mechanism, has attuned it in the most correct and delicate respondency with all the moralities of which human nature is capable.

"And should there be other philosophers who affirm that 'morality hath a real and substantive existence in the nature of things, so as to make it as much an object of judgment distinct from him who judges, as are the eternal and immutable truths of geometry,' let it with gratitude be acknowledged that the mind is so constituted as to have the same hold of the moral, which it has of the mathematical relations; and if this prove nothing else, it at least proves that the Author of our constitution has stamped there a clear and legible impress on the side of virtue.

"We should not exclude from this argument even the degrading systems of Hobbs and Mandeville; the former representing 'virtue as the creation of human feeling,' and the latter representing 'its sole principle to be the love of human praise;' for even they tell us thus much: **the one** that virtue is **linked** with the well-being of the community, **the** other that **it has an** echo in every bosom.

"We would not dissever **all** these testimonies, but bind **them** together into **the sum and** strength of a cumulative argument. The controversialists have lost themselves, but it is in a wilderness of sweets, **out** of which the materials might be gathered of such an incense at the shrine of morality as should be altogether overpowering. This is the contest between them—not whether morality has claims, but what, out of the great number that she possesses, **is** the great and preeminent claim on which man should do **her homage.** Their controversies, perhaps, may never be settled; but to make the cause of virtue suffer on this account would be to make it **suffer from the very force and abundance of its** recommendations.

"**But this** contemplation is pregnant with another inference, **beside** the worth of virtue—even the righteous character of Him who, for the sake of upholding it, hath brought such **a** number of contingencies **together. When we look to the** systems of utility and selfishness, let **us look** upwardly to Him through whose ordination alone it is, **that** virtue hath such **power to** prosper the arrangements of life and society.

"Or when told **that the** principle of virtue is its own reward, let us not forget Him who **so constituted** our moral nature as to give the feeling of **an exquisite charm,** both in the possession of virtue and in the contemplation of it.

"**Or** when **the** theory of a moral sense (or faculty) offers **itself to our** regards, let us bear along with it to that God, **who** constituted **this** organ of the inner man, and endowed **it with all** its perceptions and all its feelings.

"**In the** utility wherewith he hath followed up the various observations **of** moral rectitude; in the exquisite relish which

He hath infused into the **rectitude** itself; in the law of conformity thereto which He hath **written** on the hearts of **men**; in the aspect of eternal **and** unchangeable fitness, under which He hath made **it manifest to** every conscience—in these we behold the **elements of many** a controversy in the nature of virtue; but **in** these, when viewed aright, **we also** behold a glorious harmony of attestations to the **nature of God.**"

"**It is** thus that the perplexities of the question when **virtue** is looked to **as** but **a** thing of earthly residence, are all done away, **when** we carry **the** speculation upward **to Heaven.** We find **solution there, and** cast a radiance over the character of Him who hath not only established in righteousness his throne; but, by means of a rich and varied adaptation, hath profusely shed over the universe that He hath formed, the graces **by** which He would adorn, and the beatitudes by which he would reward **it.**")

LESSON XII.

RULE OF MORAL OBLIGATION—INSUFFICIENCY OF THE LIGHT OF NATURE—THE HOLY SCRIPTURES.

58. *What do you understand by the rule or law of moral obligation?*—By the rule or law of moral obligation, I understand the rule or standard by which human conduct ought to be regulated.

59. *What is that rule or standard?*—The rule or standard by which human conduct ought to be regulated is undoubtedly the will of God.

60. *Why?*—*First*, Because the will of God is, and must ever be, like himself, holy, just and good. *Second*, Because He is the Creator and Upholder of the universe, and must, therefore, be the Supreme

Governor. I am his subject, and the workmanship of his hands. *Third,* The will or command of God is the rule of conduct to the highest orders of intelligent beings. The inspired Psalmist says, "*Bless the Lord, ye his angels, that excel in strength, that do his commandments, hearkening unto the voice of his word*" (Ps. 103: 20). Our Saviour said, "My meat is to do the will of him that sent me, and to finish his work" (John 4: 34). The rule of conduct for angels, and that which directed our Divine Redeemer himself, must be the highest rule or standard by which human conduct should be regulated.

61. *How is the will of God made known to us for the regulation of our conduct?*—The will of God is made known to us for the regulation of our conduct by express revelation in the Bible. "Holy men of God spake as they were moved by the Holy Ghost" (2 Peter 1: 21). "All Scripture is given by inspiration of God, and is profitable for doctrine, for reproof, for correction, for instruction in righteousness; that the man of God may be perfect, thoroughly furnished unto all good works" (2 Timothy 3: 16, 17).

62. *But may not the light of nature, without the Bible, teach us the will of God—what God would have us do, and what he would have us avoid?*—The light of nature teaches the will of God in many things; but the light of nature was created when man was innocent and holy, and not since he became guilty and sinful; and the light of nature teaches only by

observation and experience, and not directly and orally, as does the Bible, which not only teaches all that is taught by the light of nature, but what the light of nature never taught, and cannot teach—namely, the immortality of the soul, the existence of a future state, the way of salvation through Jesus Christ, and the doctrines and institutions taught by our Lord and his Apostles in the New Testament.

(NOTE ON THE TEACHINGS AND INSUFFICIENCY OF THE LIGHT OF NATURE.—The light of nature is another phrase for natural religion. It teaches much respecting what are called the natural attributes of God—his eternity, wisdom, power, knowledge, benevolence—but **nothing as to his** holiness, **justice**, mercy, **truth**; nor anything as to the character and condition of man. "The heavens declare the glory of God, and the firmament showeth his handywork" (Psalm 19: 1); but observing ever so minutely, and admiring ever so profoundly the power and skill of an architect, gives us no insight into his moral character, much less does it acquaint us with his will in regard to others. The laws of nature, including that of man's physical and moral **constitution, are the** order of God's government, **and thus far the** expression of his will. When we violate any **of** those **laws, we** experience certain **consequences, from which** we may infer what God's will is **respecting such acts.** For example, **He** has connected happiness **with certain** actions, and misery with certain others, **by** causing us to feel pain of conscience when **we do** some things, and pleasure of conscience **when we do** other things; pain and misery of body and mind with gluttony and drunkenness; abhorrence **of** the **liar** and thief; wretchedness in families where parents **are cruel,** intemperate, or lazy, or children are disobedient, **abusive and quarrelsome with** each other; the impossibility of a community existing, composed of liars, drunkards, thieves and murderers. From this connexion between bad actions and bad consequences, **may** be inferred the will of **God** that **we** should avoid such actions; and from the good consequences following many good actions, may **be** inferred **the** will of God that we should perform **such** actions. Such is the teaching of natural religion; but how uncertain, inefficient and feeble is the voice of such teaching? What parent would leave his children **to learn** his will and their duty from observing the consequences **of their** conduct? What government would leave its **ambassador** at any foreign court to infer his **duty** from **his knowledge** of the character and views of the government that sent him, or from considering the consequences of his acts? Even the late Royal Commission from England to Washington waited for instructions from its Government in regard to every article of **the treaty it was** engaged in negotiating. A nation—if **such can** be conceived—has never left its individual citizens to ascertain their duty by **each** observing **the** consequences of his own conduct, and **acting** accordingly; but it has enacted laws for common protection, **and for individual** guidance and warning in all that relates to the public welfare. Much less has the Father of the families **of the earth** given **existence** to a world of children, and **then** abandoned them **to their own** speculations and fancies **as to** their duty and happiness. He has given them his Word, as "a lamp unto their feet, and a light unto their path" **(Psalm 119:** 105), and that Word is able to make them "wise unto **salvation"** (2 Timothy 3: 15).

LESSON XIII.

THE TEACHING OF THE BIBLE SUPERIOR TO THAT OF NATURAL RELIGION IN TWELVE PARTICULARS.

63. *Wherein is the teaching of the Bible superior to that of natural religion?*—The teaching of the Bible is superior to that of natural religion in all respects.

1. While natural religion teaches "the eternal power and Godhead" of Jehovah (that is, his eternity and omnipotence), and but dimly his other natural attributes of immutability, omnipresence, omniscience and benevolence; natural religion teaches us next to nothing of God's moral attributes of mercy, justice, truth and holiness, with which we are so immediately concerned.

2. Natural religion teaches nothing as to the present fallen state, guilt, depravity and moral helplessness of man; nor of the truths most essential for the formation of religious character, and for the possession of a firm hope of immortality.

3. Natural religion teaches us nothing respecting the duration or even existence of a future state, much less of a future state of retribution.

4. Natural religion teaches us nothing as to the means by which sin may be pardoned, or as to the way of salvation by Jesus Christ.

5. No system of religion, professedly derived from the light of nature, has rendered men professing it perceptibly better.

6. Wherever men have lived without the Bible, they have been vicious; and the more they have advanced in knowledge and refinement, without the Bible, the more corrupt and vicious they have become, as in the case of ancient Greece and Rome.

7. But on the contrary, as the God of revelation is the God of nature, the Bible teaches all that

natural religion teaches; and teaches it, not by the speculations and inferences of reasoning beyond the habit and capacity of the masses of mankind, but, by the express declarations of Jehovah, plain to the understanding of a child.

8. The Bible teaches the character of Jehovah; not only his natural attributes of eternity, immutability, omnipotence, omniscience and wisdom, but his moral attributes of holiness, justice, truth and mercy, on which natural religion sheds not a single ray of light.

9. The Bible teaches the causes of man's present sinfulness, guilt and misery, and how his sins may be pardoned, his sinful nature made holy, and his misery changed to happiness; respecting all which natural religion teaches nothing whatever.

10. Natural religion knows nothing of man's existence or state beyond the grave; nothing of the resurrection of the body; nothing of the future judgment and its results. The Bible alone teaches man his immortality, his resurrection from the dead, the general judgment, and brings all the revelations and sanctions of eternity to bear upon the occupations of time.

11. The doctrines of the Bible respecting God and man, time and eternity, man's responsibility, and the method of his pardon and purification, form the principles of the man, and constitute the essential elements of moral character. Lord Bacon says: "As a man thinketh in his heart, so is he." To be

virtuous, a man must possess virtuous principles; as his principles, so **is the man.** Moral principles constitute the seed, of which moral character is **the** fruit. A man's morality must take its rise from his **principles.** A man's principles are himself, as is his morality; and the Bible alone teaches **the** doctrines which **are** to morality what **the fountain is to** the perennial stream, or the heart **to the** living man.

12. The Bible furnishes **the** only infallible **rule** and **authoritative standard** of right and wrong. The **rule** of **Bible morality is the** will of God, and its standard is the character **of** Jehovah. The sum of its moral teaching is, "Be ye *holy*, for I the Lord your God am *holy*." God is holiness; God is love; God is truth; God is rectitude; God is justice; God is mercy. How different a character this from that **of the** incestuous Jupiter, the revengeful Juno, and the lascivious Venus—the chief objects of Pagan worship, and standards of Pagan morality!

.

LESSON XIV.

HOW WE KNOW THE BIBLE IS THE WORD OF GOD; TEN REASONS IN PROOF OF IT.

64. *How do you know* **that the** *Bible is the* **word** *of God?*—I know that the Bible is the word of God just as I know that you, and not **another person,** have asked **me** this question—just **as I** know that thunder is the voice of God in nature, and not that **of man.** The Jews **said, in regard to our Lord and**

Saviour, "never man spake like this man" (John 7: 46); so never book speaks like the Bible. I seem to hear the voice of God in it, as I hear and know the voice of my own earthly father when he speaks to me, even when I do not see him.

65. *But the Bible was written many ages ago?*—So was the sun created many ages ago; but it shines as brightly to-day as it did the first morning of its existence.

66. *But how do you know that those who wrote the Bible were taught or inspired by God to write it?*—*First*, Because men could not write such a book of themselves, any more than they could make the world.

Secondly—Because, as I do not know your mind and will unless you make it known to me, so we cannot know the mind and will of God unless he communicate it to us.

Thirdly,—Because He who made man, and made man capable of communicating with him in various ways, can himself communicate with man in whatever manner he pleases, whether by word of mouth, by writing, by angels, by visions, by dreams, or by signs.

Fourthly—Because the holy prophets and apostles who wrote the Bible professed to have been taught to do so by the Holy Spirit of God.

Fifthly—Because the doctrines and morals which they taught are not only superior to what had ever been taught by the most learned philosophers and moralists of their ages, but are as far superior to any doctrines and morals that have ever been taught by any uninspired writers of any or of all countries down to the present time, as the light of the sun is superior to any other light produced by the ingenuity of man.

Sixthly—Because the writers of the Bible did not write for any "private interpretation," or for any selfish and personal purposes, like false pretenders, but for public warnings, encouragements, and instruction, as occasion required.

Seventhly—Because the predictions of the Bible in regard to ancient cities, and countries, and nations, including the nation of the Jews, have been and are being fulfilled in the histories of those cities, countries and nations to this day: so that any one who wishes can take the Bible in one hand, and in the other hand the histories of all the ancient cities, countries and nations mentioned in the predictions of the Bible, and he will find in the narratives of the former the most complete fulfilment of the prophecies of the latter, though most of them were uttered and written more than two thousand five hundred years ago.

Eighthly—We have equally sure records of history to prove the truth and fulfilment of the predictions of the Old Testament prophets respecting the time, place and circumstances of the birth of our Divine Redeemer, his character, life, ministry, miracles, crucifixion and resurrection; the propagation and effects of the gospel through the preaching of the Apostles and their successors.

Ninthly—There are thousands and hundreds of thousands of living, as well as millions of departed Christians—including men of the highest rank, scholarship, science and statesmanship—whose testimony would be above suspicion in any court of justice, who have testified, and do testify, in sickness and in health, in adversity and in prosperity, in life and in death, that the gospel of Jesus Christ, received by the penitent and believing heart, is invested with more than human power, in the pardon of sin, in the renewal of the heart, in the renovation of the life, in the purification, courage and comfort of the mind, in the hope of a glorious hereafter—is, indeed, in all these respects, "the power of God unto salvation."

Tenthly—We know that those who pretend to reject the Bible have no certain standard of faith and morals, if they have any of either; having nothing but the shifting sands of expediency, and that blown about by every wind of passion, as the rule of their practice; are irregular in life, and miserable in death, as their greatest modern apostle, Voltaire, said in his dying hours,—"I am abandoned by God and by man."

LESSON XV.

MIRACLES—FALLACY OF HUME'S OBJECTION TO THEM EXPOSED.

67. *You have mentioned* MIRACLES. *Are not miracles contrary to the experience of mankind, and how can any amount of testimony counterbalance such experience?*—That cannot contradict experience respecting which there is no experience, any more than knowledge contradicts the ignorance which it removes by teaching. Mankind generally may have had no experience of miracles, but those had who witnessed them, and they have borne testimony to what they have experienced. Mankind never experienced or knew at all the wonderful powers of a composition of saltpetre, sulphur and charcoal into a little black powder, called gunpowder, until two centuries ago; mankind had no experience until the present century of the power of an invisible agent called steam, produced by the application of heat to a visible liquid (water), to propel vessels across the ocean against both wind and waves, and carriages by land at the rate of fifty or sixty miles an hour; nor, until the present generation, had mankind any experience of the possibility, much less reality, of an invisible agent to convey instantaneously, by means of a metallic wire, human thought from one side of a continent, and even of the ocean, to the other. Yet not one of these and many kindred facts, entering so largely into the interests and practice of national, commercial and social life, could be proved by any amount of testimony, if there be any foundation in the objection of expe-

rience to miracles repeated by so many superficial and thoughtless persons since the days of its inventor, *David Hume*, who justified the most vicious practices, while he doubted his own existence. Multitudes, who know nothing of astronomy, believe, on the testimony of astronomers, that the earth moves round the sun once a year, and round its own axis once in twenty-four hours; multitudes, who know nothing of the means of ascertaining a ship's longitude or latitude, cross the ocean in full faith in the testimony of others that both can be ascertained and the ship safely steered to the destined port; multitudes who never experienced the effects of arsenic, firmly believe it to be a poison on the testimony of others, and act accordingly.

68. It is true, nothing appears more unreasonable and absurd, when you come to analyze it, than Hume's oft-repeated objection to miracles; *but is the the testimony borne to miracles such as to justify your unwavering faith?*—I have stronger evidence on which to ground my faith in the miracles and works of our Lord and his Apostles, than I have to believe in the existence and character of the emperor Julius Cæsar; for I have the testimony of both sacred and profane historians to the reality of the former, while I have only the testimony of profane historians as to the history of the latter. Take for example the miracle of our Lord's resurrection from the dead—the sum of all the other miracles—the miracle which forms the corner-stone of the edifice of Christianity itself. It is agreed by both the friends and enemies

of Jesus Christ, that he was crucified—that he was buried—that precautions were taken against the violation of his tomb, in consequence of his having predicted his resurrection—that the third day after his death his body had disappeared from the tomb. His enemies asserted that his disciples stole his body from the tomb while the Roman guard of forty soldiers slept; his friends asserted that he rose from the dead, according to the predictions of the ancient prophets, as also according to his own predictions. In regard to the story of the enemies of Jesus Christ, three things are to be observed:

First—If the guards slept, they could not testify what took place while they slept. No court of justice would credit the testimony of a man as to what occurred while he was asleep.

Second—The soldiers were not punished for the confessed crime of being asleep on guard, though the Roman law imposed certain death for such a crime. The case, therefore, breaks down on both these grounds; and the natural inference is that the story of the guard being asleep was a pretence, and the story was got up by the enemies of Jesus Christ by bribing the soldiers, assuring their justification and escape, in order to justify their crucifixion of the Son of God, and continued hostility to his doctrine and disciples.

Third—This is further confirmed by the facts, that no inquiry was instituted to discover the guilty parties in stealing the body of Jesus, nor as to the alleged conduct of forty soldiers being asleep and all asleep during a watch that included only about three or four hours, and early in the morning, so that the soldiers might have slept before; that the Jews never afterwards repeated this fabricated story of Christ's body having been stolen from the tomb while the Roman guard of soldiers slept—never on any subsequent occasion denied the resurrection, any more than the crucifixion of Christ, when asserted by the Apostles and early disciples of Christianity; but their whole opposition to the Gospel was based upon the allegation that it was in opposition to the law and institutions of Moses.

Then, on the other hand, take a mere summary of the evidence in support of the great miracle of our Lord's resurrection.

First—It was predicted by Jewish prophets several hundred years before its alleged occurrence.

Second—It was predicted by our Lord and Saviour himself, in connection with his prediction of his crucifixion, as necessary to fulfil the predictions of the prophets and to accomplish the great work of human redemption.

Third—Had not Jesus Christ risen from the dead, according to those predictions, his disciples would have been the greatest sufferers from the failure and the most interested in exposing it.

Fourth—The disciples of Christ, both men and women, declare without exception, that they saw and conversed with him at different times after his resurrection; that he gave them the most tangible proofs of his identity; and that he was seen by no less than five hundred of them at one time.

Fifth—Not one of these disciples ever recanted this testimony, but evinced their adherence to it and reliance upon it by lives of purity, self-denial, labour and suffering; and many of them sealed their testimony by a death of martyrdom.

Sixth—The disciples of Christ openly declared, as eye-witnesses, his resurrection in Jerusalem itself within fifty days after it took place, and when there were some two or three millions of strangers from all countries assembled there on the occasion of the greatest national festival of the Jews.

Seventh—The disciples of Christ appealed to ocular demonstration and experience in confirmation of his resurrection, declaring that in consequence of it the influences and gifts of the Holy Ghost had been granted, and the power of working miracles had been conferred upon themselves; and as illustrations of these mysterious and supernatural influences and gifts, three thousand persons were converted from hostility to discipleship, from guilt to pardon, from distress to joy, from vice to virtue, in one day, and gifts were bestowed, so that among persons speaking nearly twenty different languages, every man heard them speak in the tongue wherein he was born "the wonderful works of God" (Acts 2: 1–11). The Apostles of Christ wrought various other miracles in Judea and other countries, in confirmation of their testimony, as recorded in the Acts of the Apostles, written by St. Luke, during the age of the Apostles, and which would have been exposed at once had not its statements been true, but which was never contradicted by any contemporaneous or ancient author.

Eighth—The establishment of so many Christian congregations, the conversion and reformation of so many thousand individuals of all ranks in various provinces of the Roman Empire during that age (admitted by all historians), are so many corroborative and confirmatory testimonies to the resurrection of our Lord, and the supernatural effects of its propagation.

Ninth—The establishment and observance of two institutions, which have existed among all Christian peoples and nations from the Apostles' to the present time, attest beyond all reasonable doubt the fact of our Lord's resurrection—namely, the institution of the Lord's Supper and the observance of the Christian Sabbath; the former having been instituted to commemorate our Lord's death, in connexion with his resurrection, until his coming again, and the latter expressly observed to commemorate his resurrection. Ignatius, a contemporary of our Lord and his Apostles, a martyr to his belief, in a letter to the Philadelphians, the genuineness of which has never been disputed, not only says "Christ truly suffered, as he truly raised up himself; I *know* that after the resurrection he was in flesh, and I believe him to be so still," but says, "Let every one that loves Christ keep holy the Lord's day, the queen of days, the resurrection day." Theophilus, a Christian father, about sixty years later, says, "Both custom and reason challenge us that we honour the Lord's day, seeing that on that day it was that our Lord completed his resurrection from the dead." Says Clement of Alexandria, thirty years later, "Christians, according to the command of the Gospels, observe the Lord's day, thereby glorifying the resurrection of the Lord." Thus there is no fact of ancient or modern history which is confirmed by such abundance and variety of conclusive testimony as the resurrection of our Lord; and the marvel is, that any one can doubt it.

69. It would be incredible that any sane person could doubt our Lord's resurrection, did we not see men, blinded and impelled by passion, act every day contrary to fact and reason. *But is there not a great mystery in our Lord's resurrection?*—Yes; not only our Lord's resurrection, but everything that we do not comprehend, is mysterious to us. It is so, not because there is anything contradictory or doubtful in it, but simply because it is beyond our comprehension. Many things which are done by parents or grown-up people, are mysterious to children; and many things which are a mystery to untaught and ignorant people, are quite plain to men of science; such as the power of steam, the ascent of a balloon, the motions of the heavenly bodies that cause the

changes of the seasons and the succession of day and night. But in the works of an *infinite* God, there are and must be many things which are beyond the comprehension of any *finite* mind, and therefore mysterious to it. We know there is a principle or power within us by which we feel, and by the volition of which we open and shut our eyes or mouth, or move a hand or foot; but how this is done, or what this power or principle is, we know not; it is an impenetrable mystery to us; yet we believe it, and act upon it every day of our lives. Nothing is more foolish and absurd than to disbelieve or doubt a thing because it is mysterious to us, since, in such a case, we should disbelieve our own existence, and the existence of everything around us, as it is all profoundly mysterious, being beyond our comprehension. "Without controversy, great is the mystery of Godliness" (1 Timothy 3: 16); because its greatness and grandeur, its glory and its blessedness, surpass all that the eye hath seen or the heart conceived, and is lost in the effulgence of the Sun of Righteousness.

(NOTE ON THE INFIDEL'S OBJECTION TO BELIEVE WHAT IS MYSTERIOUS.—Nothing is more common with the infidel than for him to say, "I am not bound to believe what I do not comprehend;" and upon this superficial and absurd ground of objection he professes to deny the doctrine of the atonement and other doctrines of the Christian religion. Take our Lord's own illustration of the cause, the mystery, the results of his death and resurrection. He says (John 12: 24), "Except a corn of wheat fall into the ground and die, it abideth alone; but if it die, it bringeth forth much fruit." In these words, employed by our Lord in teaching the necessity and objects of his death and resurrection, he compares *himself* to a *grain of wheat;* his **death** to the *death* and *decomposition* in the ground of the grain of wheat sown; his *resurrection* to the *blade* which springs up from the dead grain; the *results* of his death in the salvation of men to the *fruit* which the grain thus dying brings forth.

Now, **why wheat** should not have been produced except through this process of death, **we know** not; all we know is, that it has pleased God to attach the multiplication of wheat to the death and decomposition of the grain in the earth, and **to produce wheat in no other way;** so it has pleased Him to attach the **redemption of a lost** world to the death of our Lord Jesus Christ, and in no other way, declaring that "there is no other name under heaven given among men, whereby we must be saved" (Acts 4: 12).

Next look at the *mystery* of this process, **which we must believe without being able to** comprehend it. Take first **the illustration, and then the truth** illustrated. The illustration is, the multiplication of a grain of wheat, and, I may add, our nourishment **by its** reception as food into our system. We know as facts, as physical truths, that the whole **body of the** grain dies, is converted into **fine earth, which** forms the first nourishment of **the embryo plant,** and prepares it **to receive a grosser support from the** surrounding soil; we know also that **nothing lives but the** *germ*, **which** is included in the body of **the grain, and which must** die also, if it receive not from the **death** and putrefaction of the body of the grain nourishment, so as to enable it to unfold itself. These are **facts which come within our** observation, and which **we can comprehend;** but **no philosopher that ever lived, or that now lives,** has been able to explain, **or can** explain, **how** one grain of wheat becomes **thirty or sixty grains;** how **a** grain of wheat **vegetates** in the earth; **how earth, air and water,** its component parts, assume such a form and consistence, emit such odours, **or** produce such **tastes. Nor can the wisest philosopher** tell how our animal **bodies are nourished by this produce of the** ground; **how** wheat, when taken as food, in the form of bread or otherwise, is assimilated to the very bodies that receive it, and becomes bones, sinews, arteries, veins, nerves, flesh and blood. All we know and all we can say is, that it has pleased God it should be so, and not otherwise; but mystery, inexplicable and incomprehensible mystery, meets us at every step of the process; yet every farmer believes in this mystery, and shows his faith by his works in agriculture; and every sane man believes in the mystery of nourishment by the bread of wheat, and shows his faith by his works in receiving food.

So, in regard to the great truth illustrated by the above facts and mysteries in vegetable and animal physiology. Though there are many things relating to the person, death, resurrection, sacrifice of Christ, which may not be explained or comprehended, any more than many things relating to the multiplication of a grain of wheat, and its nourishment of our bodies; yet it has pleased God, in the one case as in the other, that it should be so, and not otherwise. Though the body of our Lord died, there was still the *germ*, the quickening power of the Divinity, which reanimated the body, and stamped the atonement with infinite merit, or with merit infinitely *multiplied;* so that through the death and resurrection of that one person, the man Christ Jesus, united to the eternal Word. (John 1: 12), salvation is provided for a world of sinful men; and as the material bread by which we are nourished is procured by the death of the grain, so the spiritual food by which we are nourished unto everlasting life, is procured by the death and resurrection of our Lord Jesus Christ. "Thus it is written, and thus it behoved Christ to suffer, and to rise from the dead the third day; and that repentance and remission of sins should be preached in his name among all nations, beginning at Jerusalem" (Luke 24: 46, 47). "It is Christ that died, yea rather, that is risen again, who is even at the right hand of God, who maketh intercession for us" (Rom. 8: 34).

The young as well as the old Christian can take and abide in this truth to his great comfort, knowing that as the body is mysteriously nourished by grain mysteriously multiplied, so the soul is nourished by the imperishable bread of Christ's body from heaven; for He himself hath said, "I am the living bread which came down from heaven: if any man eat of this bread, he shall live forever: and the bread that I will give him is my flesh, which I will give for the life of the world" (John 6: 51).

NOTES ON THE BIBLE.—ITS CHARACTER—ITS INFLUENCE UPON THE INTELLECT AND HEART—ITS EXCELLENCE. — To what has been said in questions 61-66, on the Bible as the rule of faith and practice, its inspiration and teachings, may be added the following remarks: Dr. Cumming well observes, "In looking over the whole Bible, we find the following data: It contains in all sixty-six books, by forty different writers. It presents history, biography, parables, letters, proverbs, poems, speeches. Some of them were written by kings, some by shepherds, some by herdsmen, some by vine-dressers, some by tent-makers, some by a physician. They were composed in different circumstances, in successive centuries, in various phases of joy, of sorrow, of affliction, and of tribulation. Between the first writer in Genesis, and the last writer in the Apocalypse, fifteen hundred years intervened. Now, must we not conclude, in the exercise of common sense, that in men of so varying professions, placed in so varying circumstances, subject each to his peculiar and idiosyncratic trials, there is evidence of special inspiration, when we find that, without collusion, there is perfect concord; without preconcert, perfect harmony; that without design or adjustment, their notes, not from nearness, but relation, should constitute the varied harmonies of heaven? Is it not evidence that there must have been struck, to guide and to develop them, one grand key-note, Christ, and him crucified? In one part of this wondrous book the scholar is addressed in language so exquisitely, in thoughts so freshly drawn from the depths of human experience, that he listens, and admires as he listens. In another part, the weary artizan, who has returned from his day's work, hears the voice of his

Father, and finds that voice his noblest opiate, his sweetest lullaby. In one part, the Bible speaks to babes; in another part, it speaks to grown men. It draws its imagery from agriculture, from commerce, from politics, from poetry, from nature, and from art; so that there is not a human being, however strange and peculiar his taste, who shall not find in this wonderful book the common Christianity conveyed in those formulas and figures, and illustrated by those analogies which come home to his heart with the greatest emphasis, and convey most vividly the great truths that belong to his everlasting peace. If a shepherd wants to read his Bible, he will find allusions that will make it familiar to him as household words; if a king sits down on his throne to read the Bible, he will meet with illustrations there that are meet for the inmate of the largest and most splendid palace; if the farmer, or the artizan, or the sailor, or the soldier, read the Bible, he will see the same truths illustrated by imagery with which he is practically familiar, and so coming home to his heart with a power so real and so decided, that he will feel that never book spake like this book, as it was said of old of its Author.— 'Never man spake like this man.'"

2. The Bible is the best book in the world for both the *intellect* and the *heart*. The mind is enlarged and invigorated by coming into contact with superior minds and with great truths. If the society of wise men tends to make one wise; if by studying and mastering the great truths of natural science, especially of astronomy, the mind is enlarged and invigorated; so, in reading the Bible, we come into contact with the mightiest intellects, and with truths more lofty and sublime than those which the naturalist ever taught, or the astronomer ever conceived. The mind becomes contracted and dwarfed by daily familiarity and exclusive dealing with small things, and without ever making the effort to take the span and altitude of great facts and majestic truths. "But (as a late writer forcibly remarks) if it be for the enlargement of the mind and the strengthening of its faculties, that

acquaintance should be made with ponderous and far-spreading truths, it must be clear that knowledge of the Bible outdoes all other knowledge in bringing round the result. We deny not that great effects may be wrought on the peasantry of a land by the wondrous diffusion of general information which is now going forward through the instrumentality of the press. But if a population would be made a Bible-reading population, it would be a far more thinking, and a far more intelligent population, than it will ever become through the turning its attention on simplified sciences and abbreviated histories. The Bible would be going a vast deal farther towards making them strong-minded and intellectual, than the dispensing among them treatises on all the subjects which philosophy embraces. The Bible, whilst the only book for the soul, is the best book for the intellect. The sublimity of the topics of which it treats; the dignified simplicity of the manner of handling them; the nobleness of the mysteries which it developes; the illumination which it throws on points the most interesting to creatures conscious of immortality; all these conspire to bring round a result which we insist upon as actual and necessary—namely, that the mind which should study the Bible, and not be benefited by it spiritually, would be benefited by it intellectually. We think it may be reckoned amongst incredible things, that converse should be held with the first parents of our race; that man should stand on this creation whilst its beauty was unsullied, and then mark the retinue of destruction careering with a dominant step over its surface; that he should be admitted to intercourse with patriarchs and prophets, and move through scenes peopled with the majesties of the Eternal, and behold Godhead himself coming down into humanity, and working out, in the mysterious coalition, the discomfiture of the powers of darkness;—we reckon it, we say, amongst incredible things, that all this should be permitted to a man—as it is permitted to every student of Scripture—and yet that he should not come back from the ennobling associations with a mind a hundred-fold more expanded, and a hundred-fold more elevated, than if he had given his time to the exploits of

Cæsar, or poured forth his attention on the results of machinery. We speak not thus in any disparagement of the unparalleled efforts to make knowledge accessible to all classes of the community. We are far enough from underrating such efforts; and we hold, unreservedly, that a vast and a beneficial effect may be wrought amongst the poorest classes, by the well-applied agency of vigorous instruction. In the mind of many a peasant, whose every moment is bestowed on wringing from the soil a scanty subsistence, there slumber powers which, had they been evolved by early discipline, would have elevated their possessor to the first rank of philosophers; and many a mechanic, who goes patiently the round of unvaried toil, is, unconsciously, the owner of faculties which, nursed and expanded by education, would have enabled him to electrify senates, to win that preëminence which men award to the majesty of genius. But we only uphold the superiority of scriptural knowledge, as compared with any other, when the alone object proposed is that of developing and improving the thinking powers of mankind. In all the wide range of sciences, what science is comparable, in its sublimity and difficulty, to the science of God? In all the annals of human kind, what history is there so curious, and so riveting, as that of the infancy of man—the cradling, so to speak, of the earth's population? Where will you find a lawgiver from whose edicts may be learned a nobler jurisprudence than is exhibited by the statute-book of Moses? Whence will you gather such varied illustrations of the power of truth, as are furnished by the march of Christianity, when the Apostles stood alone, and a whole world was against them? And if there be no book which treats of a loftier science, and none which contains a more interesting history, and none which more thoroughly discloses the principles of right and the prowess of truth; why then just as far as mental improvement can be proved dependent on acquaintance with scientific matters, or historical, or legal, or ethical, the Bible, beyond all other books, must be counted the grand engine for achieving that improvement: and we claim for the Holy Scriptures the illustrious distinction, that, containing whatsoever is needful for saving the soul, they present also whatsoever is **best** calculated for strengthening the intellect."

3. But it is upon the *heart*—the seat of moral character, the source of feeling and affection—that the Bible, in its instrumentalities, truths and precepts, exerts the loftiest influences and effects the noblest achievements. The application of scriptural truth to the heart and conscience by the almighty agency of the Holy Ghost, will, whilst it gives an unwonted vigour to the intellect, exalt and purify the affections; making the exercise of *love* pervade all our duties; placing before the affections an object and standard of perfect purity and loveliness in the character of our Heavenly Father; and thus forming wisdom, strength and beauty of character, instinct with the highest elements of happiness in ourselves and of usefulness to others.

4. I conclude, therefore, in the eloquent and impressive words of the late Henry Melville: "Of all the boons which God has bestowed on this apostate and orphaned creation, we are bound to say that the BIBLE is the noblest and the most precious. We bring not into comparison with this illustrious donation the glorious sun-light, nor the rich sustenance which is poured forth from the storehouses of the earth, nor that existence itself which allows us, though dust, to soar into companionship with angels. The Bible is the development of man's immortality, the guide which informs man he may move off triumphantly from a contracted and temporary scene, and grasp destinies of unbounded splendour, eternity his lifetime and infinity his home. It is the record which tells us that this rebellious section of God's unlimited empire is not excluded from our Maker's compassions; but that the creatures who move upon its surface, though they have basely sepulchred in sinfulness and corruption the magnificence of their nature, are yet so dear in their ruin to Him who first formed them, that he hath bowed the heavens in order to open their graves. Oh,

you have only to think what a change would pass over the aspect of our race, if the Bible were suddenly withdrawn, and all remembrance of it swept away, and you arrive at some faint notion of the worth of that volume. Take from Christendom the Bible, and you have taken the moral chart by which alone its population can be guided. Ignorant of the nature of God, and only guessing at their own immortality, the tens of thousands would be as mariners tossed on a wide ocean, without a pole-star and without a compass. It were to mantle the earth with a more than Egyptian darkness; it were to dry up the fountains of human happiness; it were to take the tides from our waters and leave them stagnant, and the stars from our heavens and leave them in sackcloth, and the verdure from our valleys and leave them in barrenness; it were to make the present all recklessness, and the future all hopelessness—the maniac's revelry, and then the fiend's imprisonment — if you could annihilate that precious volume which tells us of God and of Christ, and unveils immortality, and instructs in duty, and woos to glory, Such is the Bible. Prize it, and study it more and more. Prize it, as ye are immortal beings—for it guides to the New Jerusalem. Prize it, as ye are intellectual beings—for it 'giveth understanding to the simple.'")

LESSON XVI.

HAPPINESS.

70. *In what do all mankind agree as to the great end of their lives?*—All mankind agree to seek happiness as the great end of their lives. Whether rich or poor, learned or ignorant, old or young, of whatever nation or country, every human being is seeking happiness as his ultimate end.

71. *Wherein do mankind differ in regard to happiness?* —Mankind differ in two essential things in regard to happiness: they differ as to its *nature*, or in what it consists, and as to the *means* of attaining it.

72. *How do they differ as to the nature of happiness?* —Some make happiness consist in riches; others in high stations; others in the pleasures of sense; others in exemption from all labour and toil; others again believe true happiness consists in the favour and image of God; the former as the cause of our happiness, the latter as the disposition and qualification to enjoy it—both producing a relation and character of being in which there is the least pain, the highest exercise of the faculties, and the fullest gratification of the desires.

73. *Why do you think that happiness does not consist in riches?* —I think that happiness does not consist in riches, for several reasons: 1. Because our Lord himself has said, "A man's life consisteth not in the abundance of the things which he possesseth" (Luke 12: 15); the plain meaning of which is, that our life is sustained by little, and does not need abundance for either its support or its comfort; and therefore we are counselled and warned in another place, upon the same divine authority, that "having food and raiment, let us be therewith content. But they that will be rich (that is, they that are resolved, above all things, upon being rich) fall into temptation and a snare, and many hurtful lusts, which drown men in destruction and perdition" (1 Tim. 6: 8, 9). If man's happiness consisted in riches, such words could not have been employed by Him who knows what is in man. 2. Riches, while uncertain in themselves, add nothing to the certainty or length of man's life, but often stain and shorten it by the vices of indolence, intemperance and luxury; and the anxiety and fear of death, or of a change of fortune, are much more painful to a rich man than to any other. 3. Riches do not cure or alleviate any of those inward disorders of the mind from which the greatest human troubles originate—the guilt of our consciences, the vicious inclinations of our wills, the irregularity and disorders of our passions. No bad man—no man under the control of bad passions—can be happy, though he possessed the whole world. 4. Riches increase the wants and cares of their possessor, more than they minister to his happiness; cares which are greatly enhanced in the case of the covetous man who digs, and labours, and pinches himself to heap up riches—thus becoming a beggar for himself, and rich only for his heir, or heirs, who may waste and scatter his riches in extravagance and vice faster than he has accumulated them. 5. When a man who has sought his happiness in riches, comes to die, nothing can exceed his distress and misery. 6. Riches increase the difficulties to their possessor of "entering into the kingdom of God," though the proper use and benevolent application of them may greatly increase both his usefulness and enjoyments, and enable him to convert what, from its misuse, is usually called "mammon of unrighteousness," **into** " friends " that will " receive him into everlasting habitations."

74. *Why does not happiness consist in the pleasures of sense ?*—The pleasures of sense—by which I mean **the** animal gratifications of eating, drinking, sensuality, and various amusements, &c.—cannot make their devotee or victim happy: *First*, Because they are short-lived; and the more short-lived they are, the more gross. When the actual sensation of such pleasures is computed, it will be found that they occupy a very small portion of the twenty-four hours. *Second*, They lose their relish by repetition; blunt and benumb the organs of their perception; disappoint expectation; create in those who pursue **them** " a restless and inextinguishable passion for **variety (as Paley says), a** great part of **their** time being vacant, **and much of** it irksome; **so that** with whatever eagerness and expectation they set out, they become by degrees fastidious in their choice of pleasures, languid in the enjoyment, yet miserable under the want **of it."** *Third*, **These** pleasures often undermine health and **ruin** fortune, producing the perpetual irritation **of** enfeebled health and embarrassed circumstances. *Fourth*, The retrospect **of such pleasures** affords no satisfaction to their most ardent devotees, who are rendered destitute by extravagance and the decay **of** faculties, tormented by desires that **can** never be gratified, and by the memory of pleasures which must return no more.

75. *Why does not happiness consist in exalted rank or station ?*—There are several reasons why happiness cannot consist in exalted rank or station; amongst which I will give only the following: Those who have been raised to the highest stations and greatest power, have not been happy. Their cares, and often their desire for more honor, or power, or wealth, or all these together, have increased in proportion to their advancement. David, though a good man, was probably not so happy as a king, as he had been as a shepherd. Ahab, king of Israel, with all his power and riches, was as avaricious of Naboth's vineyard (1 Kings 21: 1-4), and as unhappy without it, as many a covetous man is who has a farm of two hundred acres, unless he can add another fifty acres to it, and even then he would wish further additions to his possessions. Haman, the prime minister of Persia, had no enjoyment of his greatness and wealth, as long as Mordecai, a Jew, would not uncover his head and bow down to him as he passed into the royal palace (Esther 5: 9-13). Louis Napoleon, late emperor of France, was not happy in possession of his great empire, unless he could get a slice from the kingdom of Prussia, so as to extend his eastern territories to the Rhine, and for which he made war that lost him his empire and reduced him to exile. Perhaps the good Queen of the British Empire has as much anxiety for her children as any mother in Canada for her children; and has, perhaps, more care, if not more trials and vexations, than the humblest of her subjects.

76. *Why does not happiness consist in exemption from all labour and toil?*—Happiness does not con-

sist in exemption from labour and toil for three reasons: *First*, "Such a state of being (as Paley says) is usually attended, not with ease, but with depression of spirits, a tastelessness in all our ideas, imaginary anxieties, and the whole train of hypocondriacal affections. For the same reason, persons who retire from business or active life, to spend the remainder of their days in leisure and tranquillity, seldom realise their expectations, and soon die or return to some active pursuit." *Second*, Activity is an essential element of happiness; and a man derives far more enjoyment from the exertion of his active powers in the midst of toils and efforts, than he can from a life of indolent and selfish indulgence, and a total abstraction from the concerns and duties of the world. An inactive and slothful person must endure the constant pain of despising himself, as well as of being despised by others. *Third*, The stagnation of both the bodily and mental faculties, like stagnant water, breeds disease and corruption throughout the whole moral man, which almost invariably issues in vice, degradation and ruin.

77. *In what then do you think happiness consists?*— I think that happiness, which is a state of mind and of heart irrespective of outward circumstances, consists or is made up of several elements, which are essential both to its attainment and enjoyment.

1. There must be moderation or reasonableness in our expectations. In our present life, happiness is comparative and imperfect. To expect too much is to insure disappointment and discontent. A person

is called happy in comparison with another, or in comparison with himself in another situation, or when the aggregate of his enjoyment exceeds that of pain or discomfort; but perfect happiness appertains not to a state of imperfection, danger, affliction and mortality, and must not, therefore, be expected in the present life.

2. *A second element of happiness is the exercise of the social and benevolent affections.*—Man is born for society; and the play of the social affections, in being surrounded by objects of endearment, as in the domestic circle, or with companions, produces cheerfulness and enjoyment; while peevishness and lowness of spirits attend the recluse and solitary. The exercise of the benevolent, no less than of the domestic and social affections, refreshes the spirits and produces grateful and pleasurable emotions, in acts of sympathy, kindly counsel, and bounty to the afflicted, the unfortunate and the needy. In enjoyment, no less than in duty, it is "more blessed to give than to receive."

3. *The exercise of our faculties, both mental and bodily, is the third element of happiness.*—A human sloth is an unhappy as well as despicable being; but the exercise of our faculties in pursuing an engaging end—"something to hope for and look forward to"—produces an elevation of spirits, a real enjoyment, which contrasts strikingly with the dejection and *ennui* of those who do nothing, and have nothing to hope for beyond what they possess,

though they may even possess wealth and rank. It is this intolerable vacuity of mind which carries many to the race-course, the gaming-table, and other vices, which both corrupt and destroy; while active engagement in pursuit of some lawful object —as acquiring a language or a science, or application to our calling for family support and competence, or planning laws and institutions, or devising schemes for promoting charities, or agriculture, or manufactures, or commerce, or even "raising a cucumber or a turnip,"—contributes to both enjoyment and virtue. Engagement and industry are everything; and the more noble and lofty the objects pursued, the better. It is thus that things divine and eternal rise in worth and grandeur infinitely beyond those of time, expand the mind, prompt to activity, and elevate our hopes and enjoyments in their pursuit.

4. A fourth element of happiness is the formation and maintenance of *good habits;* habits of early rising, of temperance, of industry, of economy, of honesty, of purity. This is one great secret of human happiness. A habit once formed becomes easy, and a sort of second nature. Bad habits are a bondage and misery; good habits are self-mastery and freedom, a continual source of inward satisfaction and cheerfulness, and conducive to success and prosperity: and it is said, even in respect to fortune, that "it is not the income that a man possesses, but the increase of income that affords pleasure." Good habits also contribute to *health*—another element of

happiness. It was the counsel of Pythagoras — "Choose the course of action which is best, and custom will soon render it most agreeable."

78. *But are there* **not other and** *higher elements of happiness?* — Yes; the primary and ever-living spring of true happiness is the **Being of** all possible perfections and blessedness; and the consciousness of His favour and conformity of heart to His image of righteousness and true holiness, must be the highest state of enjoyment, as well as of honour, to which any human being can be exalted in this life.

79. *Why do you think so?* — I think **so for the following reasons:**

1. Because **such** a state and character approaches **most closely to that** in which man was originally created, when he **was** both holy and happy.

2. Because such **a** state **and** character **involves** the purest and noblest exercise of all our faculties, whether of mind or body, and therefore contributes in the highest degree to health and happiness.

3. Because the feelings, dispositions and habits of such a state **and character are** most exempt from **the** fear, tempers and passions which render us most unhappy: a sense of pardon, instead of condemnation; filial **love** to God instead of guilty enmity against him; delight in holy works instead of sinful **works**; devotion instead of profanity; temperance instead of intemperance; industry instead of idleness; virtues instead of lusts; good-will to men

instead of envy and hatred against them; meekness and forbearance instead of anger and strife; contentment and resignation to God's will and appointments instead of discontent and murmuring; ambition and desire for eternal honours and wealth rather than for those which are temporary and perishable; fellow-labour and companionship in joy with the holiest men and greatest benefactors of this world, and the spirits of the just made perfect and angels in heaven, rather than fellowship with wicked men and their wicked works; the moral image and heirship of God rather than the highest intellectual attainments and greatest earthly possessions without God.

4. Because the possession and practice of true religion,—which is only another word for such a state and character—with its hopes and expectations, exerts the most satisfying and beneficial influence on the mind in youth, in health, and in prosperity, as also in age, in sickness, and in adversity; making duties pleasures, creating undecaying sources of consolation; giving freshness and vigour to the powers of the mind and affections of the heart as years increase. "Its influence outlives all earthly enjoyments, and becomes stronger as the organs decay, and the frame dissolves; it appears as the evening star of light on the horizon of life, which, we are sure, is to become, in another season, a morning star; and it throws its radiance through the gloom and shadow of death."

www.ingramcontent.com/pod-product-compliance
Lightning Source LLC
Chambersburg PA
CBHW032244080426
42735CB00008B/991